# HOW TO PLAY THE
# GAME OF YOUR LIFE

# HOW TO PLAY THE GAME OF YOUR LIFE
## A GUIDE TO SUCCESS IN SPORTS—AND LIFE

by George A. Selleck, Ph.D.

Diamond Communications, Inc.
South Bend, Indiana
1995

# HOW TO PLAY THE GAME OF YOUR LIFE

Copyright © 1995 by George A. Selleck, Ph.D.

*10 9 8 7 6 5 4 3 2 1*

Manufactured in the United States of America

Diamond Communications, Inc.
Post Office Box 88
South Bend, Indiana 46624-0088
Editorial: (219) 299-9278
Orders Only:
1-800-480-3717
FAX (219) 299-9296

Library of Congress Cataloging-in-Publication Data

Selleck, George A. (George Abraham), 1934—
    How to play the game of your life : a guide to success in sports-
-and life / by George A. Selleck.
        p.   cm.
    ISBN 0-912083-80-8
    1. Success. 2. Sports--Psychological aspects. 3. Athletes--Life
skills guides. I. Title.
GV706.55.S45   1995
796' .01--dc20                                                95-6808
                                                                CIP

# CONTENTS

### PART ONE
### BEFORE THE GAME: UNDERSTANDING THE SPORTS EXPERIENCE

### PART TWO
### DURING THE GAME: LEARNING FROM THE SPORTS EXPERIENCE

# FOREWORD

I'm glad someone has finally created a how-to book about sports that deals fully and honestly with life after the game is over—as it inevitably has to be for every athlete.

Dr. George Selleck is a man who is uniquely qualified to write such a book, as he so powerfully proves on every page of his *How to Play the Game of Your Life*.

These are the reflections of a sports man, a true man of sports, who knows the score, both on the playing field and off. His hard-won insights come from nearly five decades in the sports arena, first as a college athlete, then as a coach and referee, and now as an adviser to countless sports organizations, including the NBA.

What he has to say is of vital interest to everyone who has any involvement with athletics. Particularly those who parent and coach athletes, or who are administrators.

To make his book even more valuable, Selleck has broadened its scope with a wealth of references and testimonials that just about anyone can relate to and be helped by.

If sportsworld participants had had access to the information provided in this book and had the opportunities to utilize the personal game plans presented by Selleck, we would hear and read many less stories about athletes who have fallen upon hard times.

This book does not suggest that people should feel sorry for those athletes who have had both success and problems at different levels. Nor does it attempt to get one to view, with sadness, those who have tried but failed to reach their goals; Selleck will have none of that.

*How to Play the Game of Your Life* is a pragmatic book that can help give direction to people who are caught up, or know others who could get entangled in, the marvelous world of sports, to the neglect of all else that would give their life survival balance.

I would further like to add that Dr. Selleck's book has an appeal that reaches far beyond the world of sports. It is fascinating, valuable reading for everyone who has ever competed for anything, anywhere, anytime. And that includes just about all of us.

*Tom "Satch" Sanders*
*Vice President, Player Programs*
*National Basketball Association*

# ABOUT THE AUTHOR

The telephone at my San Francisco home rang early one morning, brutally early. By the time I got the instrument to my ear, the man on the other end, a complete stranger to me, was in mid-sentence.

Meet George Selleck.

George Selleck has been many things to many people over his 60 years on the planet: Athlete, coach, counselor, minister, corporate executive, husband, and father. Most of all, he is a man who lives life with an uncommon passion.

A New York book editor, Rick Wolff, likes to joke that George is the only person on the West Coast he can telephone first thing in the morning. One morning five years ago, Wolff could have phoned me. I was up, awakened by a caller with a voice and a name I did not recognize.

The man said he was writing a book and that something in my newspaper column that morning led him to believe I was the person to help him write it. He said his name was George Selleck and that he'd played basketball at Stanford in the 1950s. He offered me his credentials and listed John Wooden and Pete Newell, famed West Coast college basketball coaches, as references.

Not more than a week later, a box of yellowed press clippings arrived at my home, special delivery.

Selleck was "the Bob Cousy of the West," according to one of his contemporaries, Phil Woolpert, the coach who guided the great University of San Francisco teams of Bill Russell and K.C. Jones. Russell himself called Selleck "the biggest little man in basketball"; those were the words Russell scribbled above his autograph in the program for the 1956 College All-Star Game at Madison Square Garden, a game in which Selleck played alongside Russell, Jones, and UCLA's Willie Naulls. (The East team featured a high-scoring forward from Holy Cross named Tom Heinsohn.)

Selleck was only 5' 8" and 140 pounds, and three major operations on his right leg had left him without a knee cap.

Still, he was the high school player of the year for Southern California in 1952, when he led Compton to a 32-0 record. He was a three-year standout at Stanford—back then, collegiate careers were limited to three years—and he became only the third player in school history, following Ron Tomsic and Hall-of-Famer Hank Luisetti, to net 1,000 points. To this day, Selleck remains among the Top 20 in school scoring. He was inducted into the Stanford Hall of Fame in 1958.

For all of his success, though, Selleck says his sports experience was neither enjoyable nor educational. And that is why he has written this book: To help show athletes, of all ages and every level of success, how to get the most from their sports experience, both in terms of enjoyment and personal growth.

I must confess to having abandoned this project several times over the years. George, obviously, did not.

The same wellspring of determination that made him a star athlete despite his size and physical handicap, the same doggedness that allowed him to excel in competition against bigger, stronger men, the same indomitable spirit that carried him through recent surgeries for cancer and a heart ailment—those are qualities that made this book a reality.

Every few months for the past five years, a new manuscript, thicker and improved, has arrived at my door. Every few days, the telephone rings early in the morning.

Meet George Selleck, author and friend.

*Bud Geracie*
*Columnist, San Jose Mercury News*

# PREFACE

In June of 1994 this manuscript was in its last stages (or so I hoped), and I was relaxing by watching Game 5 of the NBA Finals. Suddenly, the game was interrupted by a special news bulletin, and I found myself transfixed by the spectacle of a white Ford Bronco sailing down the Los Angeles freeways with a bevy of police cruisers bringing up the rear.

O.J. Simpson was on his way home.

I had, of course, been following the headlines just like everyone else. There was the initial shock of hearing about the murder of O.J.'s ex-wife, Nicole, and her friend Ronald Goldman. Then there was the biggest shock of all—learning that O.J. was about to be arrested for this brutal, horrible crime. O.J., who on the surface seemed to be a textbook example of an athlete who successfully made the transition from the sports world to the real world, instead turned out to be a better example of one who may not have.

As columnist Nick Canepa wrote in the *San Diego Union*, "No one was surprised when Mike Tyson was convicted of rape, or when Pete Rose was banned from baseball for gambling or even when Michael Jordan was thought to have a gambling problem. But O.J. Simpson, murderer/fugitive? As news, this is syrup of ipecac. Your body tries to reject it. It tries to throw it up. Because he was one of the last great American heroes…"

But with each succeeding news story, I was saddened to learn that O.J. was not so heroic, after all. Rather, he was an athlete who moved in a special world, with all the perks and concessions that went with fame and talent. He was an athlete who had no difficulty meeting women, but a lot of difficulty maintaining a successful relationship with them. He was an athlete whose talents off the field never quite equaled those on the field. He was an athlete like many of those I write about in this book, who failed to learn the lessons of sports, the lessons that can help build life skills and promote personal growth.

As I write this, the trial has not yet taken place. We may yet learn that O.J. Simpson is innocent of murder. But we'll never again think of him in the same way. Guilty or not, O.J. has lost his innocence…and to a great extent, so have we.

The only thing that remains is to try to make something positive come of this whole tragedy. Hopefully, one of those "positives" will be an increased awareness of the crime of domestic violence. I would also hope that we could become more aware of the way we treat our heroes—the ways we insulate them from effectively dealing with their problems. Finally, I hope that this will help every young athlete realize that being a successful athlete, even being one of the greatest ever, will not exempt you from the same kinds of challenges and setbacks that everyone else faces.

Just ask O.J.

# ACKNOWLEDGMENTS

As a point guard, I was always looking for a way to "get it done" on the court and put my team in the best position to win. It has been no different with this team effort.

This book's vision of helping athletes to become "winners" in the game of life as well as in sports would not have been possible without:

*My good friend, mentor, and former Stanford teammate, David Epperson, who seldom misses a day or opportunity to encourage and support my efforts;*

*Rick Wolff, one of several new friends I made on this journey, who simply wouldn't let me "quit" in the face of the usual setbacks that someone experiences in preparing a manuscript for publication;*

*My wife Randie, who had to "put up" with hearing about this project for "too many" years, but whose support and encouragement were always available;*

*My children, John, Alison, and Peter, who have watched their father "grow up" with compassion and love and who have always been my inspiration and driving force;*

*Jill and Jim Langford, editors and publishers of Diamond Communications, Inc., who quickly have become family and are just what Rick Wolff said they were, "good people";*

*For their ideas and time I'd like to thank John Wooden, George Winch, Mariah Burton Nelson, Judith Hollard, John Robinson, Ted Leland, Doug Stamm, Mike McKee, Tom Davis, Rudy Washington, Michael Robinson, Bud Geracie, Bill Shaiken, Robert Khayat, Tom "Satch" Sanders, Gary Cunningham, and Don Sabo;*

*And, Wendy Fayles, whose valued writing contributions I wish to recognize with deep appreciation.*

*My Inspiration*

*Randie Selleck • John • Alison*
*Peter • Mark • Tomasa • Keith • Alexis • Jessica*
*Dave Epperson • Ann Martel • Beth Hahn*
*Marianne Frase • Rick Wolff*

# INTRODUCTION

*Walk softly as you tread forward;*
*you just might tread on my dreams.—Keats*

In February 1957, while I was struggling with "what now?" following my student/athlete days at Stanford, a physician in nearby Santa Rose, California, phoned me. He had this patient, a former star athlete, who, at the time, was trying to "get his life in order" after a long bout with the bottle. My doctor friend thought that the companionship of someone who'd lived the "sports life," who could relate to this patient's glory days, might be therapeutic. He gave me his name. "Star athlete" had not begun to describe him. A few days later, I left my fraternity house and moved in with a legend.

Ty Cobb had played—epitomized—major league baseball for 24 years before retiring in 1928. His career totals in hits and stolen bases ranked him No. 1 on both all-time lists well after his death. Cobb won the American League batting title every year from 1907 to 1919 (except for a 1916 "slump" when he batted a mere .371). To this day, his lifetime batting average of .367 stands as the major league record. In short, Cobb was a legend, an original Hall-of-Famer and, arguably, baseball's finest all-around player.

In the months I shared with him in a large, rambling house in Menlo-Atherton, the hours and hours we spent talking about his career and disappointments, what stuck with me, more so as the years turned to decades in my own life, was how he wrestled, at age 70, to make sense out of life. Baseball had given him fame, notoriety, money, but it hadn't brought happiness, sense, or meaning to the life he struggled through after his last at-bat.

Today it seems as if everywhere you look the lives of athletes are unraveling. Witness the headlines:

"Len Bias Dies of Overdose"
"Athletes Involved in Dorm Shooting"
"Tyson Convicted on Rape Charge"
"Baseball Players Charged in Theft"
"Coach Fired for Recruiting Violations"
"Magic Johnson Has AIDS Virus"

"Rose Jailed on Gambling Conviction"
"Kendall Charged with Manslaughter"
"Harding Investigated in Kerrigan Assault"
"Capriati Arrested, Facing Drug Charge"
"Simpson Charged in 2 Slayings"

No wonder an increasing number of people today decry the role that athletes and sports play in American life. Some simply issue a blanket condemnation of sports for the failed lives behind the headlines. But I think such a view is too simplistic.

Sports have been a part of my life since childhood. I found my identity growing up on the basketball courts of the interracial community of Compton, California. In 1952, *California* magazine picked me as "High School Basketball Player of the Year." Four years later, I played in the '56 College All-Star Game alongside future Boston Celtics Bill Russell and K.C. Jones. Basketball was such a pivotal experience in my life that, 35 years later, I've yet to shake it. To some extent, I still see myself as a ballplayer who happens to be a management and sports consultant rather than someone who once played basketball and is now a psychologist turned consultant.

Having been around sports all my life, first as a player, then as a coach, referee, and parent, I know that the athletic experience can enrich one's life in ways nothing else can. So why don't all athletes discover the same thing? What happens to rob athletes—regardless of their level of achievement—of the riches gained through sports?

In the winter of 1988, I worked in the San Francisco Bay area during the week and most weekends drove home to San Diego and my family. All that time on the road gave me a chance to think deeply about the personal troubles of sports stars such as Pete Rose, Wade Boggs, and Steve Garvey. What had happened? The stories all seemed to boil down to the same thing: athletes were losing in *life*, the one game that mattered. And the question persisted—Why?

I bought some solace in the form of a season pass to Stanford basketball. I attended home games and relived my glory days on that same court. All that I loved about sports shone in the bright faces of those Stanford players.

Still, I wondered how many of those bright faces would end up dimmed in some future sports front page? Or enter old age, like Ty Cobb, haunted by the days when the eyes, passions, and hopes of a stadium crowd, or the world, focused on them?

In spite of the all-too-common stories of tarnished stars, drugs, sex, labor strife, NCAA violations, and scandals, many youngsters still dream of championship seasons, world bests, and coming back from the brink to beat the odds. This, despite the fact that there are no sure things. Witness the stories of Bob Gulaskey and Curtis Bray.

Bob was a high school star gifted with a 91 miles-per-hour fastball and a .500 batting average. He knew he was destined for the big leagues. The Pittsburgh Pirates suspected it as well, drafting him in the 34th round. Bob said good-bye to college scholarships and welcomed the dream—the very one that lured a young Ty Cobb, generations before.

Bob's pro reality lacked the longevity of Cobb's, however. In a year, his athletic career was over. So, too, were the scholarship offers from prestigious colleges and universities. Sports had been Bob's life. Now, that life had ended before it had hardly begun. Without scholarship help, Bob couldn't afford to attend a four-year college. Instead, he obtained an associates arts degree at a technical institute and began working on submarines for the military. Cutbacks in defense spending made this a tenuous job, however.

Curtis Bray also seemed destined for the big-time. A veteran of three high school All-American teams and a Gatorade Player of the Year, Curtis' professional career was a sure thing. Until the injuries began. For Curtis, though, his life didn't turn into a nightmare. As he said, "I'll definitely go to a camp if it's offered, but if it doesn't happen, it's not heartbreak city. It was never really a dream. My dad and my uncles played professional football and I knew how much guesswork it is."

"Guesswork" translates into very high odds. According to the NCAA, 70 out of every one million high school athletes will make the pros. Of those 70, most will never see a fifth season. As Ty Cobb knew, success in "The Show" doesn't guarantee success in the rest of your life. But try pushing that through a kid full of the dream. Twelve times more blacks grow up to be lawyers— and there are 15 more times more black doctors—than become professional athletes. Still, many poor or working class youngsters, particularly males (though, as opportunities grow, increasingly females, too), regardless of ethnicity, believe the athletic field is their best chance at achieving the bigger, American Dream of rags-to-rich's success.

Sports, thus, are the center of their young lives. All of their satisfaction grows from that center and, as a result, other interests wither and atrophy. Unfortunately, should the dream die if they get injured, have a performance slump, or simply lack the talent to reach the top—the consequences can be catastrophic.

Whether the inevitable end comes in high school, college, or after many successful years as a professional, too few athletes are prepared to let go of the dream. It certainly was true for me.

Sports, though it taught me a lot about teamwork, discipline, and hard work, could have taught me much more had I had young Curtis Bray's awareness of the balance between the life-long game and the games measured in quarters, periods, innings, or rounds. Any athlete who fails to grow and develop as an individual through his or her sports experience will end up living moments instead of a life and will have missed the wonderful mentorship that only sports can provide.

Ty Cobb flunked those lessons. His character development never equaled his tremendous athletic growth. Life isn't about whether you can reverse dunk or pitch a no-hitter. It's a celebration of who you are and what you have done with your given time. It's what you can do when the dreaming stops and you must face the world wide-awake.

When I first began writing this book, I focused more on elite athletes who had managed to make a career of sports, as they came to the end of that career. I thought I would write something that would help these athletes in their transition from the sports world they lived in for so long, to the real world that would become the rest of their lives.

Then I realized that the book needed to be addressed to all athletes, not just stars. Because the message isn't so much about how to "get over" sports and get on with your life as it is about how to get the most out of the athletic experience—whatever that experience consists of. It was about using the lessons sports teach to help succeed in the bigger and more important game of life.

The goal of this book is to help all athletes—the serious and weekend amateur, the will-bes and wanna-bes—positively shape their sports experience, regardless of the extent of that experience. I'll share stories of athletes who traded successfully one dream for another. People who made the transition from the sports world to the real world by remembering what sports had taught them as persons.

You'll meet athletes as well who have struggled with that transition and learn why it was so hard for them. And, along the way, you'll learn the Zen of athletics—the teachings sports give us that transcend sport and inform life. Finally, you'll see how to apply these lessons in your life, whether on the field, in the classroom, on the job, or in relationships with others.

This journey didn't begin for me in 1988 with headlines and their resulting questions of how one "survives" success in sports. Neither did it start with me sitting across a table from a sports legend, listening to him speak of his zenith from his twilight in 1957. It all began in a place and time I cannot really fix. Somewhere in the Compton of my youth, on a sun-drenched day, watching young men bounding between two hoops, giving life to ball and stirring a dream.

This book, hopefully, is neither about the end of journeys nor of dreams. Rather it should be a beginning of new ones.

# USING THIS BOOK

It is best to read a book cover-to-cover. You may, however, be drawn to a particular chapter because of some urgent issue in your life. Or you may have read the book but wish to review a chapter here or there. I've structured *How to Play the Game of Your Life* so that it can be used fruitfully as a reference book as well as an "easy read."

First, the contents page can lead you to areas of interest. Second, each chapter of the book begins with a brief "Game Plan" that simply outlines the points of the chapter. "Game Plans," just like a sports game plan, focus you on what's coming.

Finally, most of the chapters conclude with "Practice Time"— exercises designed to help you avoid or get out of some of the traps you may see yourself in after reading the chapter. Like sports practices, they are essential if you are to be successful in transferring your sports skills to life skills. You must be as dedicated in these practices as you are in sports. Particularly in areas where your skills are weak and need to be strengthened.

*Then strip lads and to it, though sharp be the weather*
*And if by mischance you should happen to fail,*
*There are worse things in life than a fumble on heather*
*And life is itself but a game of football.*
                              —*Sir Walter Raleigh Scott*

# PART ONE
## Before the Game:
## Understanding the Sports Experience

# 1
# THE SPECIAL WORLD OF SPORTS

## The Game Plan

In this chapter, I'll discuss elements that make the sports world exciting, alluring, challenging, and different from anything else an athlete ever experiences. These elements include:

- the drama
- the publicity
- the physical strain
- the short career span
- the special treatment
- the dumb jock stereotype

### *You begin to feel like Louis XIV.*

#### - Wilbur McClure, two-time Golden Gloves champion

Few things in America are more popular than sports and few people are more popular than athletes. The athletic world, with its physically superior inhabitants, huge salaries, fame, and adoring fans, seems like the ultimate dream for millions of young people.

Without doubt, the world of the athlete is unique. Whether your athletic "career" begins and ends with a couple of seasons in Little League or takes you to the top ranks of the professional athlete, the experience you gain in the sports world can influence the rest of your life.

Some of those influences will be positive. Some will be less so. Many of the things you learn from sports will depend on the attitudes and actions of those around you, including parents, teammates, coaches, administrators, and fans. But much of it depends on you.

All learning begins with understanding. If you are to learn from sports, you need to first understand the world that athletes inhabit: the drama, mythology, and extremes that turn a simple game into a multi-million dollar business, an average group of fans into a borderline lynch mob, and an ordinary human being into a god.

## The Drama of Sports

*We imagine all politicians as crooks, all businessmen as con men. But sports offers us, well, sportsmen, a word that has far greater connotations than just the ability to run and jump and throw.*
  - Art Spander, sportswriter


*Sports is this place that we like to think is pure, whereas the rest of society has been corrupted. It's a place where clear rules apply. There is always black and white. There is a winner and a loser.*
  - Steven Stark, commentator for National Public Radio


*I read the sports pages first, because they record man's accomplishments. The front pages record their failures.*
  - Chief Justice Earl Warren


When Reggie Lewis died on the basketball court after being diagnosed with a heart ailment that might prove fatal if he played again, one writer said that "for some reason, basketball was too intoxicating a lure for Lewis to resist."

The Boston Celtics star was not alone in finding sports irresistible. The triumphs and tragedies that occur during the course of a sporting event are reminiscent of ancient Greek drama with its god-like characters facing life-or-death challenges in front of a crowd of adoring spectators.

Greek dramas don't fixate us anymore. Instead, we have "Monday Night Football." In place of a stage, we have an athletic field on which dramas containing many elements of traditional theater are performed.

The drama of sports is something that affects the players as much as it does the fans. Dr. Arnold Beisser, a psychiatrist who has counseled athletes, noted that "for many athletes who are 30 or 35 years old, there is no field that will ever be as fulfilling, even if they conscientiously try to prepare for a career."

When Pat Riley resigned as coach of the Los Angeles Lakers, he said it was going to be hard to find something that would give him the same jolt as basketball. Apparently, he didn't find that "something"—because he soon signed on as coach of the New York Knicks.

Willie Davis, a former Green Bay Packer who went on to become a successful businessman, once said that all the excitement of owning a business and being recognized in the business community for his achievements still couldn't quite fill the void left by football. "You played because you wanted to see the joy on a fan's face," Davis explained. "It was the romance of the fans in Green Bay." For the athlete, that kind of romance is hard to duplicate elsewhere.

There is another element of sports that's hard to duplicate. As Kevin Cobb wrote in an article on sports relationships [*First*, April 5, 1993] "...sports offer that rarest of experiences in life: conflict *with resolution.* Every game has a beginning, a middle, and an end. And at the end, there is a winner, a loser, and a final score. Compare that to other life experiences—work, marriage, family relationships. How often do you have absolute resolution there?"

There are no subtleties on a scoreboard. Things are either black or white, win or lose. You always know exactly where you stand. In today's turbulent society, that can be a very comforting feeling. And so we turn to sports—for excitement, for inspiration, and for security.

## Glass Houses

*It's obvious, folks, that our lives are parallel to yours—the joys of success, the agony of defeat—the difference is we live our lives out on the public stage, often with unqualified and unauthorized judges deciding whether the job is done well or not. We have high profiles and live in glass houses, but we laugh, cry, hurt, and worry the same as you do.*
- John Lucas, referring to his career as a guard in the NBA

*Because you're in the public eye, people are always gushing over you, telling you how great you are and all that mushy malarkey. They want my autograph. My autograph! For what? Maybe I'm a jerk, maybe I'm a heel. How do they know? They just see me play basketball.*
- David Cowens, former star player and coach for the Boston Celtics

*You think you know somebody because you sit next to him in a locker room or you see him on TV or you live on his block. But you don't know all of him.*

- Tony Kornheiser, columnist, *Washington Post*

When O.J. Simpson was charged with the murder of his ex-wife and her friend, the public recoiled. We had seen him so much—playing football, running through airports, in the commentator's booth, on the movie screen. He always seemed so nice, so approachable, so *genuine*. Arresting O.J. was like arresting a member of the family. No wonder people cheered him, even as two people lay brutally murdered.

We like to have heroes. Heroes make us feel better about ourselves. They make us feel better about the human race, in general. So we look for heroes to emulate and to dream about, and the athletic field is one of the first places we look.

That's where Damon Bailey was found. In the late 1980s in Bedford, Indiana, Damon Bailey was a household word. What did he do to earn such an honor? Find a cure for cancer? Save a child from a burning building? No. Damon played basketball. *High school* basketball. When he was in the ninth grade, women were already asking for his autograph. Even Bobby Knight, Indiana University's famed basketball coach, stopped by to watch the young freshman play. At 17, Bailey couldn't even take his girlfriend out for a hamburger without attracting crowds. As a senior, he led his high school team to the state championship before a crowd of 41,046—the largest ever for a high school basketball game. His performance led him to be chosen Basketball Player of the Year by *USA Today*, and to be named Indiana's "Mr. Basketball" for 1990.

This world sounds exciting. It is, but that excitement comes with a price tag. "The attention is something you can enjoy," Bailey once said, "but it can get old. The one thing people in Bedford won't allow me to be is an ordinary 17-year-old."

One of the perks of becoming a successful athlete is being in the public eye. One of the drawbacks faced by a successful athlete is being in the public eye. The public does not allow athletes to be ordinary. Being an athlete means that in some way you are different, that you have a physical ability or drive that is beyond others. But that single extraordinary trait can be magnified under the public microscope until it permeates every area of your life. As an athlete, you are expected to do more than just perform well. You are expected to win, both on the playing field and in other aspects of your life. If you don't, the public can be quick to turn on you. As one sportswriter said of former baseball superstars Jose Canseco and Darryl Strawberry, "They had to swing huge, drive fast, sneer at every scrape. Their bravado was awesome, so long as they averaged 30 home runs. To average less—to average much, much less—was to invite humiliation from a smirking nation."

John Thompson, Georgetown University's basketball coach, noted that, "The public perception of athletes is that they are sports heroes who can, or should, do no wrong. It's all distorted, because any sports hero like that is a fantasy like Paul Bunyan was a fantasy. And yet sports heroes give up their right to be wrong. That's wrong, but that's a fact."

To insulate themselves from these high expectations, some athletes develop a cocky, callous attitude that tells the world they can't be affected by what others think. Other athletes retreat, not letting their emotions or thoughts show. Either of these attitudes can cause serious problems.

For many athletes, the publicity that follows sports success is a Catch-22 situation. On the one hand, the excitement of the fans and the attention of the media are part of the drama of sports. On the other hand, that excitement and attention sometimes become unwelcomed—even dangerous. Following the 1993 championships for the Dallas Cowboys and Chicago Bulls, fans in both cities "celebrated" with such exuberance that three people were killed and hundreds injured. After Columbian soccer player Andres Escobar accidently put the ball into his own goal (leading to a 2-1 loss to the U.S. in the 1994 World Cup), thugs in his hometown of Medellin gunned him down, reportedly saying, "Thanks for the [wrong] goal."

When the UCLA basketball team wasn't doing as well as boosters expected, some prominent boosters went so far as to give the chancellor's office a list of coaches they would prefer to see in the job. "[Sport is] so important to the American public that it's hard to control," said Chancellor Charles Young at the time.

So athletes attempt to exert their own control. They refuse to give interviews. They expect others to "run interference" for them by keeping the fans and media away, or by smoothing over such unpleasant incidents as drunken driving arrests. In some cases, actions such as these are justified.

When Michael Jordan's father was murdered in the summer of 1993, there was immediate and unwarranted media speculation that the killing might have had something to do with Jordan's penchant for gambling. No one could blame Jordan for his subsequent disgust with the media's behavior.

In other cases, however, athletes are just plain unwilling or unable to cope with the everyday publicity that is part of the job of being an athlete. When one NFL quarterback refused to show up for training camp after being peeved at the fans' reaction to his poor play of the previous season, a teammate commented: "He wants the fans to leave him alone. I mean, grow up and learn a little bit. If you don't want to get into the limelight, then get out. Go be a trashman, or whatever it was he studied in school."

For better or worse, publicity goes with the territory. The more successful you are, the more publicity and pressure you have to deal with. It may not always seem fair, but it's part of being an athlete.

## The Physique Mystique

*Some meaningful numbers in the life of Hall of Famer Jim Otto, 52, a center for 14 years with the Oakland Raiders and now a bank director and Burger King franchise owner:*

| | |
|---|---|
| *18:* | *Number of times his knees have been operated on* |
| *2:* | *Number of knee replacements* |
| *35:* | *Number of times his nose has been broken* |
| *150:* | *Number of stitches he has had in his face* |
| *30:* | *Number of concussions* |
| *$440,000:* | *Cost of his back surgery* |
| *$35,000:* | *Cost of his last knee surgery* |

- "After the Applause," *Special Report*, February-April, 1990

Being an athlete means being physically gifted. It also means that the majority of your success is based on your body. All other attributes—dedication, concentration, drive, energy, competitiveness, and so forth—are useless without your physical ability. Few other occupations can say the same.

When I was in the 10th grade, I had a disease (Osgood Slaughter's) in my knees. It wasn't serious, but young athletes who have it are usually asked to lay off a season or so to give the legs a chance to develop. Instead of listening to my doctor, however, I went straight from the football field to the basketball court. Then, in one of the games, I went up for a lay-up and was hit from behind. My knee hit the wall and my leg was severely broken. It required two operations to repair the leg and another operation to remove the pin that had been holding the bones together. I was told by five doctors that my life as an athlete had just ended. "Develop some other interests," they advised.

I didn't have any other interests. So against the doctors' advice, I continued to play basketball. I even made the varsity team. Yet, as we were warming up for the very first game of the season, my leg locked. The doctors said, "We told you so."

Shortly after that, I paid a visit to my godfather, who had been head of the U.S. Army's orthopedic surgeons in World War II. He told me that he detected a bone spur on my kneecap and offered to remove it. While I was in the hospital recuperating, doctors kept parading in and out of my room, giving me much more attention than a simple bone spur operation warranted. A shy 11th grader, I hesitated to ask what was going on, but I finally got up the nerve to confront my godfather. That was when he told me that my kneecap had been totally smashed and he had removed it. My heart sank. In those days, if you lost your kneecap, that meant you had a stiff knee for life. There went my basketball career—again.

However, while my godfather had been serving in the Army, he had learned from a Swedish doctor how to remove the kneecap and retain mobility. As he explained this to me, I brightened. Maybe there was hope for me yet!

Within two days after my release from the hospital, I tried to play a little basketball. Of course, it was a crazy idea. It threatened the delicate and artistic surgery that had been performed. I ended up back in the hospital so my godfather could check out the damage and remove the blood from the vessels I had rup-tured. Amazingly, though, I hadn't messed up the surgery. Later I found out that my godfather wrote in one of the medical jour-nals that he knew, from that moment on, I was going to be a suc-cess because of my determination and desire to play.

To this day, I've never had any trouble with that knee. How-ever, what I went through is a reminder of the frailty of the hu-man body, and of how much I, as an athlete, depended on mine.

## The Shortest Season

*At 35 in sports, you're a senior citizen. But in life, you're just beginning to live.*
- Evander Holyfield, ex-heavyweight champ

As major league baseball teams prepared to begin spring training in 1994, an article in *USA Today* listed some of the play-ers trying to extend the autumns of their careers. Some of the names included: Rick Sutcliffe—age 36; Lance Parrish—age 37; Kirk Gibson—age 36; and Goose Gossage—age 42.

When you look at this list, one thing stands out. These men are very young to be looking at the ends of their careers. Even Goose Gossage, a veritable grandpa in sports years, would just be hitting his stride in the business world. Mickey Mantle ex-pressed the frustration of the athlete forced to retire at a young age when he said:

> Playing baseball is all I've ever known. It makes me kind of bitter that it's all over. You look around and see other guys my age who are just starting to reach their peak in other jobs. And I'm finished. I wouldn't trade my baseball ca-reer. But I'll tell ya, I'd give anything right now to be a lawyer or something.

As an athlete, you stake your future on your body—a body that can get sick, a body that can get hurt, a body that will even-tually get old. That's why the athletic career starts sooner and ends faster than most other careers.

Pat O'Hara learned this the hard way. An outstanding high school quarterback, Pat arrived at the University of Southern California in the mid-1980s after being heavily recruited by then-Trojan coach Ted Tollner. Instead of playing, however, O'Hara found himself spending three years on the bench behind All-American Rodney Peete. Still, Pat knew his time would come. Then, just days before his long-awaited debut as the Trojan's quarterback, O'Hara suffered a knee injury that ended his season. Freshman Todd Marinovich capitalized on the opening created by O'Hara's injury and led the Trojans to the Rose Bowl that season.

"God, I had it right here in the palm of my hand," O'Hara agonized. "Such a great team and you wait so long to play. Finally, you get the chance and it's just taken away from you."

In one survey of 100 college football players, 99 percent believed they would have a career in pro football and 87 percent didn't think their NFL career would end with a permanent injury. That's not the reality of the sports world, however. The reality is one bad break—literally—and your playing days are over.

## Forever Young

*About two weeks ago, Tim Flannery's four-year-old son, Daniel, looked up with a face filled with innocence and asked softly, "Dad, what are you going to do when you grow up?"*

*"My boy hit it right on the head," said Flannery, the most popular player to wear a San Diego Padres uniform over the last 10 years. "I've done all I can in this game. It's time to go on with my life."*

*Tim Flannery has decided to grow up.*
- from the *San Diego Union*, August 27, 1989

*If I can stay in baseball, I may never have to grow up.*
- former New York Yankee Craig Nettles, commenting on his participation in the Senior Professional Baseball Association

*Hey, you're only young once, but you can be immature forever.*
- Veteran relief pitcher Larry Andersen

Another unique aspect of the sports world is that sports is basically people playing at games. Maybe this is part of the reason some of those people never really seem to grow up.

Or maybe it has something to do with the aspect of the games themselves. Games offer immediate gratification. In anywhere from a few seconds to a few hours, you have clear-cut results. Emotional maturity, on the other hand, requires living with uncertainty and delaying gratification. Neither one of these abilities applies to sports very much.

In an unpublished research paper that was written at Harvard in 1973, sports psychologist Rick Wolff was the first to point out the extended period of adolescence that a vast number of serious athletes tend to suffer from:

> Whereas the typical adolescent goes through some sort of identity searching in one's late teens or early 20s, an athlete may find his or her so-called identity crisis postponed until the very end of his playing career. And then when that identity crisis hits—say at age 27 or 30 or older —an athlete can really find him or herself in a real dilemma.

Wolff goes on to comment that even relatively well-adjusted athletes such as Sen. Bill Bradley have found it challenging to "grow up" and leave the sports world for the real world. He notes: "Bradley always referred to the athletic experience as being in a 'tunnel of narrowing perspectives'—that is, you enter into the tunnel of sports when you're a kid and your world becomes more and more insulated from the real world—until you wake one day, find your sports career is over, and you have to leave the womb-like security of sports."

Many athletes who live in this pampered world find themselves exempted from ordinary responsibilities and from the demands of adulthood or young adulthood. In high school, teachers may excuse them from turning in homework with everybody else. Family activities more than likely revolve around their practice schedule.

In college, the special treatment continues. I can remember

arriving at Stanford University as a freshman. Registration took place in the basketball pavilion. Everywhere I looked, there were long lines—and the longest of all was for paying tuition. Those with scholarships, however, went to a special window with no line. When I walked up, the person there said, "Oh, yes, we've been expecting you." Before I knew it, all my expenses other than spending money were taken care of. A job was provided for me, whereas other people had to apply for them. Things were done for me. Throughout my life, being a basketball player has opened doors and made things easier.

The professional athlete is particularly pampered. Harmon Killebrew, a Hall-of-Famer who ran into major financial problems after leaving baseball, described the special treatment as follows: "In baseball, you pack your uniform in the clubhouse after a ball game and you see it hanging up in your locker when you get to your next city. You pack your bag and your bag gets in your room when you get to the hotel. They pay for your meals, your hotel. When you're out and you're doing it strictly on your own, it's a different situation."

Baseball player Kevin Mitchell was notorious for requiring special attention. During the San Francisco Giants' 1989 championship season, Mitchell missed several practices and team events. When he was finally fined after missing the team's first practice for the World Series, his agent excused Kevin's actions by saying the player was not "a stickler for details."

The late John Matuszak of the Oakland Raiders was another athlete people were quick to accommodate. Matuszak was a hard-drinking, hard-living man, but as long as he contributed to helping the Raiders win, ownership didn't seem to mind what Matuszak did during his off-time. In fact, Matuszak's recklessness away from the field enhanced the Raiders' image as a bunch of hell-raising bad boys. As one of the Oakland staffers said, "Basically, to be honest with you, as long as he was there on defensive day—Wednesday practice—and he was ready to play the games, the Raiders didn't worry about those things. We always had someone watching and if a guy got in a problem, we were there to help him. But we didn't care about all that stuff. We had 20 Matuszaks. Maybe not as volatile as he was, but every day somebody was doing something abnormal."

The term "special treatment" came up often in the reports on the O.J. Simpson case. In an article in *Sports Illustrated*, a former NBC sports employee noted: "He charmed his way out of any situation. Two years ago, after the AFC championship game in Buffalo, the plane was loaded and sitting at the gate when word came over the speaker: 'We'll be leaving momentarily, but we have to wait because O.J. Simpson is running a little late.' "

It wasn't just planes that accommodated O.J., however. Many felt that the light sentence O.J. received after his 1989 conviction for spousal abuse sent the message that what he did wasn't wrong—and that if he hadn't been rich and famous, he would have received a stiffer sentence. And, the final act of accommodation may have been allowing O.J. to turn himself in, instead of immediately sending police to arrest him after he had been charged with murder.

Special treatment frequently goes along with such high-visibility jobs as politician, entertainer, and athlete. Still, non-athletes usually have more time to mature and cope with the stress of a highly visible role than do athletes. The experience of being watched and applauded can begin very early for the athlete. Chris Evert, one of the all-time great tennis players, said that her world revolved around tennis from the time she was six years old. At 15, Evert turned pro and played at Wimbledon. Mark Spitz, who picked up an unprecedented seven gold medals in the 1976 Olympics at Montreal, began his swimming career at the age of eight.

"Most of these kids go out there way too soon," said Richard Williams, father of tennis prodigy Venus Williams. "They're kids in an adult world. It ain't fair. Once you go in, you can't stop it. It's impossible... But look what happens to these kids when they do go out there. Tennis kids are the worst socially developed children you'll ever see. No school. Can't spell well. Can't think well. Can't speak well. Their lives are all screwed up."

Another consequence of special treatment that many athletes speak of is the feeling that rules are meant for other people. Often, athletes think the only rules that *do* apply to them are the rules of their sport. Traffic rules, gambling rules, marital rules, rules of common courtesy—these are for everyone else.

What if Kevin Mitchell had been a sales representative for a major corporation and continually missed training meetings? Could he excuse such behavior by saying he just wasn't a stickler for details? I doubt it. If John Matuszak had been a construction worker instead of a football player, would his constant brushes with the law, alcoholic binges, and fistfights have been tolerated? Probably not.

Stephanie Cozart, John Matuszak's former fiancee, pointed out that part of Matuszak's problem was his inability to take responsibility for his own actions. "He'd say the incidents were always the other person's fault. It was never his fault. And it never had anything to do with the fact that he was high."

In the note that O.J. Simpson wrote to the public before he fled, he refused to take any responsibility for the problems in his marriage. If anything, he said the problem was that he loved Nicole "too much." In the ultimate act of denial, he said that often he had felt like a battered spouse. As Leo Braudy, the author of *The Frenzy of Renown: Fame and Its History*, explained it: "The celebrity is constantly being told how great he is by a phalanx of yes-men and supporters, so his sense of self-justification is so much stronger. In O.J.'s mind and in his so-called suicide note, he is the victim."

A famous director once said, "Eighty percent of success is just showing up." He was talking about responsibility and personal accountability—both characteristics of the mature individual. As an athlete, you know what happens when you mentally don't "show up" for a game. You lose. If you're mature about it, then you admit your mistake and ask, "What can I learn from this? What can I do to make a difference next time?" The immature, or non-accountable reaction would be to say, "Why do these things always happen to me? Boy, those refs were really out to lunch today!"

In a way, being an athlete is like being in the cradle for an extra 30 years or so. You're protected, nurtured, and cared for. It's a nice feeling. Who doesn't like being taken care of, at least once in a while? When you're an athlete, you can be forever young—at least, until the day comes when you have to step off the field and grow up.

## The Dumb Jock

*During almost any interview with a professional athlete, the dialogue can be expected to include:*

> *Reporter: When you finished school, did you have your degree?*
>
> *Athlete: No, I've got one semester left.*

*The reality is that the world of sports is a world of dropouts.*
<small>- from the *Los Angeles Times*, March 19, 1990</small>

*It requires no tabulation of statistics to prove that the young athlete who gives himself for months, body and soul, to training under a professional coach for a grueling contest, staged to focus the attention of thousands of people, and upon which many thousands of dollars will be staked, will find no time or energy for any serious intellectual effort.*
<small>- from the preface to *American College Athletics*, a Carnegie Foundation study published in 1929</small>

*My experience is that many professional athletes are bright, sophisticated, socially conscious—far from the old image of the dumb jock.*
<small>- Dr. Arnold Beisser</small>

The "dumb jock" syndrome refers to the belief that an athlete has no skills to use or contributions to make beyond the playing field. It's not just outsiders who think of athletes as "dumb jocks." Many athletes themselves feel this way. Though I graduated from Stanford University with a B+ average, I passed up professional basketball opportunities in part because I felt a need to prove that I had more to offer the world than my ability to push the ball up the court. It has taken me more than 30 years to shake the image I had of myself as a "dumb jock."

As I cover in detail the "dumb jock stereotype" and other aspects of the athlete-as-student in Chapter 5, "The Student Athlete: How Sports Teach You to Learn," I will say in general for now that the majority of athletes do not fit the "dumb" stereotype. But they may still be ill-prepared to face the intellectual challenges of life after sports.

In his memoirs, *Days of Grace*, Arthur Ashe commented:

> I had always been an avid reader, but the life of a professional athlete is not always conducive to much reflection. Athletes should be smart, but thinking too much can be a handicap on the court or on the field.

Years of passivity enforced by having someone else make your decisions for you can make you vulnerable to making poor decisions when there's no one around to help out. At the same time, poor educational opportunities can make the athlete's path to real-world success rocky. This is especially true in the case of inner-city athletes.

Many young black athletes continue to see sports as their way out of the poverty and crime that surround them. In one poll conducted by Louis Harris and Associates, a total of 59 percent of black male high school athletes expected to play ball in college, with 43 percent of those saying they could go on to a pro career. The reality is, no more than two percent of high school athletes make it in college sports; only one in 10,000 go on to the pros.

Those fortunate few who do make it to college on an athletic scholarship still have their work cut out for them if they plan to achieve either athletic or academic success. An NCAA poll of 85 Division I schools showed that of all the players who entered college in 1984 and 1985, 65 percent had failed to graduate five years later. The same poll reported that at 33 Division I schools, fewer than one in five basketball players graduated after the same five-year period.

The University of Miami, in an attempt to address this issue, has hired what are called "Hurricane Watchers," a group of students whose job it is to report to the athletic department whether football players are going to class, arriving late, or leaving early. Some people feel that this glorified form of babysitting shows the administration's commitment to educating its athletes. Others (myself included) believe it is simply another form of special treatment that robs the athletes of taking responsibility for themselves.

Not all jocks let themselves fall victim. They take charge of their own lives. Russell White could have been a first-round draft pick and an instant millionaire if he'd left school after his junior year to join the NFL. Instead, White—whose dyslexia made academics a major struggle—opted to stay at Cal and get his degree. As White said:

> I don't know what it feels like to be a No. 1 pick. I don't know what it feels like to have a million dollars. But I do know what it feels like to be a third-round pick with a college degree. And it feels good.
>
> Go around the NFL and ask how many guys have their degrees. I'm sure there's not too many. You can't play football forever, you know. People can take your money, take your job, take your car, even take your wife, but that degree, that's mine. Can't nobody take that away.

Russell White's uncle had been an NFL pro, so Russell understood better than most the enticements and uncertainties of the sports world. He used that knowledge to prepare himself to take advantage of all that sports—and life—could offer. Your goal should be to do the same.

## Practice Time

- Identify all the times you may have received special treatment as an athlete.

- Are you still receiving special treatment as an athlete? If so, how can you change this? List some specific way you can take more responsibility for yourself. For example:

  I can be sure my assignments are done on time.

  I can attend all my classes and take my own notes.

  I can begin researching possible career options by:

  - Going to the library or career center and looking up information on jobs I might be interested in.
  - Talking with a career counselor at the local college.
  - Setting up appointments to talk with people whose jobs interest me.
  - Working summer jobs in areas that I may be interested in pursuing a career.
  - Taking challenging courses instead of trying to take the easy way out.

# 2
# THE STAGES OF ATHLETIC SUCCESS

## The Game Plan

In this chapter, I will talk about:

- how the process of becoming a successful athlete can interfere with the process of maturing as an adult
- the four stages of athletic success: the Dream, the Dedication, the Payoff, and Extra Innings

*...a man's life is a succession of stages, and each stage involves its own conflicts and drama. (The major underlying problem facing many athletes is that they wish to remain "forever young," which is impossible...) Each stage is important, none is any better or more important than any other.*

*- Arthur Ashe, Days of Grace*

*She has a life now. She's married and as you get older, edge goes off. That's great for human development, but not for her as a tennis player.*

*- Chris Evert, commenting on one-time champion Tracy Austin's return to tennis*

Happy Birthday! Imagine for a moment that you've just turned 18, or 21, or whatever magical number that to you represents "adulthood." Does that mean you are now an adult? Not necessarily. Becoming an adult is not an event; it is a process.

Erik Erikson, the renowned psychologist and author, spoke of eight stages of life, which can be thought of as the steps that lead us to and through adulthood. Each stage is marked by a particular crisis to be resolved—not crisis in the sense of some gigantic problem or catastrophic happening, but rather in the sense of a turning point, a moment of transition characterized by the potential either to move forward or backward. Each stage represents certain challenges to be overcome in order to proceed along the path to maturity.

As an athlete, however, you may not go through these stages or at least not on the same timetable as your peers. In fact, you go through a different set of stages which will help you become a successful athlete, but may impede your ability to become a successful adult in the world outside of sports. Thus you may wake up one morning to find that, while physically and chronologically you're all grown up, emotionally you're still a kid.

As we examine the four stages of athletic success, your goals should be: 1) to understand the positive and negative aspects of each stage; 2) to recognize how following the path to athletic success can slow your emotional development; 3) to chart a game plan for developing as an athlete and as an individual.

## Beginning the Dream

*From the first, I was one of those kids who showed up at practice, did the hated calisthenics, learned the playbook, exhausted themselves before bedtime with push-ups and leg lifts, and hadn't a prayer...Skinny and lost within my exoskeleton of pads, dreaming Paul Hornung dreams, I faced a daily grind as a sacrificial offering in scrimmages with the first string, a spaniel among pit bulls.*

*After all these years, watching my son move through his warm-up shots with the aristocratic assurance that marks first-stringers, I found myself pushed back in time, forced to think about dreams long since put away—or so I thought.*

> - Owen Edwards, "The Son Also Rises," *Special Report* magazine,
> August-October 1989

The Dream is the glory of sports. It is the aura of the game and all that surrounds it. It's the winning and the incredible excitement it generates. It is the wonder of standing at home plate in the bottom of the ninth inning with the tying run on second base and 50,000 people on their feet, chanting your name.

Every athlete begins with the Dream. Kristi Yamaguchi, the figure skater who won a gold medal at the 1992 Olympics, said she had dreamed of the Olympics from the time she was a five-year-old girl carrying around a Dorothy Hamill doll. Johnny Bench said the same thing: "Since I was four or five years old, that's all I wanted to be, a major league baseball player. I watched

Mickey Mantle on television. He'd been like me once, a kid from a small town in Oklahoma. I wanted to be a star like him."

I can remember as if it were yesterday reading books like *The Kid From Tomkinsville* and *Fielder from Nowhere*—books that spurred my interest in sports and gave me fantasies about seemingly impossible situations where a kid from the country could wander into a baseball tryout camp and end up in the World Series. Dreams like that are still a part of me. I played basketball 38 years ago, and yet I still fantasize about getting a call from the Boston Celtics in which Red Auerbach says, "We need some help at guard. Can you come?"

The Dream begins for most athletes at a very early age. It has to. Unlike the dream of becoming a movie star or a famous writer or even president of the United States, the dream of becoming an athlete is not one that you can suddenly wake up with when you're 25. Around the age of six or so, budding athletes begin to realize they are a little faster, a little stronger, and a little more coordinated than their classmates. This realization, usually fueled by the admiration of one's family, starts providing the youngster with a solid sense of self-esteem for achievements accomplished in sports. They begin to think, "Hey, maybe I could really be good at this!" By the time the athlete has reached the sixth or seventh grade, his or her abilities are beginning to be recognized seriously by classmates. That becomes a tremendous source of pride, and an even bigger lure for following the Dream.

Male or female, super-talented or less so, basketball player, boxer, golfer, skater—all young athletes have their dreams. For some, these dreams are a pleasant way of passing the time. For others, they are a way of coping with a less than perfect world. Anthony Smith of the Los Angeles Raiders found his dream to be a way of escaping a life of drugs, gangs, and violence. When he was taken by the Raiders in the first round of the 1990 NFL draft, Smith said that it was a "dream come true."

But sometimes the Dream is a way to move everything else to the side—school, social life, relationships—and think about one thing only. Sports. When that happens, the Dream no longer enriches your life. Instead, it distracts you from the business of experiencing, growing, and maturing. Sometimes it even distracts you from the truth: that the dream of athletic success is one that comes true for only a very select few. And that you may not be one of them.

## The Dedication

*The worst thing about your dreams is sometimes they come true.*
- from "Being a Dodger Too Good to be True," the story of Billy Bean
(*Los Angeles Times*, February 27, 1990)

*I want kids and young athletes to understand that there are many temptations, many avenues out there that could be a big distraction when you get to the point of reaching stardom. But either it's going to make you or it's going to break you. You will either learn to deal with it or you will crumble.*
- Darryl Strawberry

To achieve success, you have to be dedicated. For the athlete, that dedication means making the decision to focus on athletics to the exclusion of other competing interests.

The better you get, the more dedicated you have to be. The competition gets tougher with success and you realize that talent alone cannot take you to the top. With each success comes the hunger for more. The excitement builds. So does the pressure.

Billy Bean understands that pressure. Called up from the Albuquerque Dukes to play for the Los Angeles Dodgers, Bean thought his dreams had come true. The Dodgers were his boyhood idols. But the Southern California native soon discovered the drawback of being on a hometown team. Suddenly, the phone was ringing off the hook with old friends wanting to talk about the Dodgers, wanting tickets to the games, wanting a little piece of Billy Bean. "The best way to describe it is, overwhelming," Bean said in a 1990 interview. "Here I was, always outgoing and trying to be friends with everybody, and suddenly I'm relishing my privacy. It was weird. It was terrible...[but] what separates major leaguers from minor leaguers is their ability to handle these distractions… That's the way it is, you know. You get to the big leagues. You fight for your life."

Joe Kmak was also familiar with the pressure that comes with dedicating yourself to athletic success. As a non-roster catcher for the San Francisco Giants in the late 1980s, Kmak was struggling to land a big-league job. The closer he got, the harder it became to maintain his mental focus. More and more, Kmak began to see baseball as a serious business and realized that he'd have to get serious, too, if he was going to succeed. "I told myself when the season ended I would do everything possible, in my power, to be a better ballplayer, to win a job...to prove to myself and the Giants that I can play baseball better than what I've shown in the past."

Every athlete hits this point some time, whether it be in high school, college, or the pros. This is the moment of truth, when you realize your competitors are as good as or better than you. You must either get out of the game or step up your focus and preparation one more notch in order to complete. Dedication is the quality that sets apart athletes on the verge of success from those who are equally talented but who never quite make it. In his book, *The Hundred Yard Lie*, sportswriter Rick Telander profiled a group of inner-city youth and their resolve to make it in the athletic world:

> These were high school athletes at a school where you had to make your own incentives, where failure was expected, where each day you had to ask yourself why you didn't just give in. These were the disciplined few, not the bad dudes. The boys told me how they would band together on hot Houston nights and scream at each other to keep one another from slipping into the gutter. Sometimes at the steaming summer-morning workouts they would cry from frustration. But they kept on.

No one achieves athletic success without that kind of determination. Witness, for example, the typical swimmer, gymnast, ice skater, or tennis player. To become competitive in today's athletic world, these athletes have to start reshaping their lives at age 11 or 12, in some cases, even younger.

Such dedication is admirable, but it has its price. Michael Chang became a top tennis player by the age of 17, but he had to leave school at age nine to concentrate on tennis. By the time young athletes are in their school years, their lives have been totally sheltered from the average adolescent experience. That can cause serious problems later on. While the top athlete is dedicatedly pursuing the Dream, the rest of his or her classmates are going through what Erik Erikson referred to as the "identity crisis" years—those critical years in life in which one has to search for a distinctive identity that will give one a sense of independence and competence for adulthood. It's a time for trying on different roles in life, exploring different possibilities. The athlete, however, doesn't go through this rite of passage. After all, his or her life was locked in and set on course a decade earlier.

Why pursue an athletic career when it requires so much from you? Certainly, there is the lure of the money. But I think a more basic reason is that sports give athletes a sense of well-being—a sense that you count, that you have something to offer the world. People tend to do those things that make them feel worthwhile, and sports offer that for most athletes.

In addition, the rewards for athletic success are much more powerful, immediate, and public than the rewards for being a nice kid, or getting a good grade in school. Immediate gratification is a powerful tool. Continuous gratification pushes athletes to even greater dedication and success in sports. And so you pursue victory, hoping the odds will favor you and that you will become the Michael Jordan, Janet Evans, Chris Evert, or Bo Jackson of your time.

## The Payoff

*There is a confidence and courage that comes with achievement. And the athlete in his heyday feels a fullness in mind and body that may never be equaled—though he may not know it, or consider it.*
   - Ira Berkow, *Beyond the Dream*

*There's nothing that compares to the two hours of competition... All your
senses peak. Things smell and taste better. My God, you're alive.
There's so much psyching and intimidation. There's no greater high...
People talk about the camaraderie. It's nothing compared to the juice,
the flow of the game itself. I know I'll never be able to replace it.*
- Mike Krukow, former major league pitcher

When athletes are at the top, they are truly king of their hill.
Bjorn Borg won Wimbledon five times. Jose Canseco predicted
he would hit 40 homers and steal 40 bases and then did it. For
these athletes, success was the payoff for their talent and dedication.

I remember playing against the University of Oregon during
my senior year at Stanford. It was near the end of the first half
with the score tied. Suddenly, a loose ball went rolling towards
center court and I went running after it with two Oregon players
about five yards ahead on both sides of me. I dove for the ball
and scooped it behind me to one of our players, who passed it to
another for a basket that put us ahead. The crowd came to their
feet as we played with reckless abandon to finish the half up by
eight or 10 points. That week, at the Northern California Sportswriters' luncheon (where I had been selected player of the
week), our coach described that play. He said it was the only
time in his career that he forgot he was the coach. Like all the
fans there, he had stood up and applauded. That is what the thrill
of athletics was like for me.

But athletic success has its down side, too. In 1961, Roger
Maris broke Babe Ruth's 34-year old record of 60 home runs in
a single season. It should have been an occasion for celebration.
But Maris, who lacked the charisma of the infamous Ruth, was
not a crowd-pleaser. Consequently, the fans were less than
thrilled when Maris broke their beloved Ruth's record, and they
didn't hesitate to show Maris their feelings.

Many athlete feel that success puts them on trial. Some
people seem to derive a lot of satisfaction from seeing gifted athletes fall. It's their way of saying, "No matter how great an athlete you are, you're no better a person than I am."

Athletic success brings, too, the fear that people will look at
you differently once you "make it." For the athlete who already

feels different enough, this fear can be intense. After Steve Young signed a $40 million contract with the Los Angeles Express of the United States Football League, he cried all the way home on his flight back to Provo, Utah. Young said he was afraid that all the money would change how his friends looked at him, or even worse, affect a value system that he's spent a lifetime developing.

Another drawback to athletic success is that it can reinforce the athlete's need to focus solely on his or her sport. For example, the traditional identity crisis that prompts so many college students to play "musical majors" is a process that is bypassed by college athletes. Their sense of the world is determined by what's best for their career. There is no worry about a future beyond sports. This mentality continues right into the professional years. As the competition becomes even more intense, there is even less time to worry about the "real world." Big money and one's career are now at stake, along with the culmination of childhood dreams. If anything, the athlete is more fully absorbed in sports now than at any other previous time. Even if there is a nagging concern that there is another world out there away from sports, that's the last thing the professional athlete wants to think about.

## Extra Innings

*Ted Williams parted in sweet sorrow. He homered on his final at-bat. What a sense of the dramatic. "He knew how to do even that, the hardest thing—quit," novelist John Updike reminded.*

*But it's hard, very hard. If an athlete learns anything, it is never to give up. Then, one day, he must alter his thinking—and his existence.*
- Art Spander, *San Francisco Chronicle*

*Most of life is falling-away, a gradual surrender of the dream. The reason sports provides such dramatic material is that the climax comes so early in a man's life, the decline so swiftly.*
- James Michener, *Sports in America*

*I'm back.*
> -Michael Jordan, Chicago Bulls star


*...Sandberg set a healthy precedent. He had the detachment—and the courage—to stand back and judge himself against the toughest of yardsticks. The one he set for himself. He was not content just to get by, to show up and draw his paycheck. He had something to prove every day, and when he couldn't prove it, he got out.*
> -*Washington Post* columnist David Broder, speaking of All-Star second baseman Ryne Sandberg's controversial retirement announcement in 1994

The same desire that keeps athletes reaching for the top often keeps them reaching long after they should have heard the last whistle.

Witness the emergence of the many Masters and Seniors events. At the U.S. Open at Flushing Meadow, New York, the seniors competition allows former title holders to return to the scene of past triumphs and gives tennis fans the chance to relive history. Then there was the short-lived Senior Professional Baseball Association, which prompted Richard Corliss to write in *Time* magazine, "To see a game in person is to watch 'The Natural' replayed in super slo-mo, but...only the out-takes."

But perhaps the ultimate extra-innings story belongs to ex-minor leaguer Don Johnson. The 32-year-old Johnson lied about his age to become a starting first baseman at San Bernardino Valley College. "He was just another kid like all of them," the team's coach said. "I guess baseball was such a big part of his life and this was a last hurrah."

Of course, there are those athletes who manage to defy nature and stay in the game. At age 39, Jimmy Connors was the talk of the 1991 U.S. Open for his comeback victory over Patrick McEnroe and his march into the Open's semi-finals. Said Connors, "I'm not 22 or 24 years old anymore, there's no denying that, but...you're going to have to kill me to beat me."

Change is never easy. When it means heading for the sidelines for the last time, it can be especially tough to face. As Detroit Tigers manager Sparky Anderson said, referring to players who keep coming back even when their skills have faded, "It is very hard for them to change their lives. They all really like to play. That's why they've been in the game so long." One perennial minor leaguer put it this way: "If I get sent down this time, I don't know what I'll do. Baseball is my life. It's all I've ever known." If your life has centered on sports since youth, the temptation is powerful to stick with the familiar, the comfortable, for as long as possible.

Also, as Mark Spitz noted, there's a lot of ego involved. Such was the case with Rennie Stennett, who tried to become the first major leaguer to return to active duty after five years of retirement. "Rennie is one of those people who will think he can hit forever," said Chuck LaMar, director of minor league operations for the Pittsburgh Pirates. The Pirates didn't agree. They gave Stennett a chance, but released him before his comeback bid could get off the ground.

Part of the reason many athletes hang on is economic. When you're making hundreds of thousands of dollars per year, the idea of an extra year or two packs an economic wallop. But mostly, they hang on for the sheer love of the game. After a mediocre, injury-plagued season in 1992, Dale Murphy surprised everyone (except himself) by returning for another year. Yes, the idea of one last paycheck was attractive. There was also the added incentive of needing just two homers to reach 400. But Murphy said the 400 goal was not his only motivation. "I want to be a productive player—more than just hitting a couple more homers. Every year you get to play, you appreciate it more."

The more successful you are as an athlete, the more tempting it can be to hang on just a little longer. As *Washington Post* columnist Thomas Boswell said in his book, *The Heart of the Order*:

> The better they are, the harder they fall. The greater the skill, the tighter the link to the game. The wider the fame, the deeper the addiction. The longer the career, the tougher the break. The smarter and more sensitive the nature, the deeper the wound. The greater the glory, the harder to believe that it must really end.

When Michael Jordan retired from basketball, he went out on the top of his game, and swore he'd never return. And yet, just 18 months later, he did exactly that. He certainly didn't need the money. But maybe what he did need was the magic. Just the thought that Jordan might return to the court sent a collective shiver down the spines of millions of sports fans. When you have that kind of effect on people, it is hard to turn away.

The late Lyle Alzado saw some glorious moments as a defensive end for the Los Angeles Raiders. In 1982, he was voted the NFL's Comeback Player of the Year. In 1991, at age 41, he attempted to make a second comeback with the Raiders. This time, another chance meant being able to enjoy the game again. "I'd go out and sit in the stands over the last four years and watch [the Raiders] lose," Alzado said. "I'd be in agony. I knew I could help. Finally, I decided that maybe I really could. I wanted another chance so bad." Unfortunately for Alzado, that comeback attempt was not as successful as the first. Facing the probability of not making the Raider's first cut, Alzado chose to retire.

Sometimes athletes hang on because they want to go out on their own terms. Bo Jackson underwent hip replacement surgery, then tried and succeeded in returning to baseball. Tracy Austin had her knee rebuilt with bone from her hip and returned to the tennis circuit four years after she'd left. Nolan Ryan returned to baseball in 1993 for a record 27th season. The previous season had been less than satisfying for Ryan. "I certainly don't cherish the thought of going out of my career with this kind of record," Ryan said. Instead, he ended up going out with an injured arm.

"Self-determination is what this emotional struggle is all about," said sports columnist Bryan Burwell in *USA Today*. "The great old athlete, always capable of determining the outcome of his on-field battle, simply wants to do it one more time."

When my own athletic career ended, an identity that I had spent more than 21 years developing died. My focus disappeared. Gone was the structure that kept my life organized and purposeful. Gone was the camaraderie of teammates. It was the end of a natural high. New Jersey senator Bill Bradley, a former all-star forward for the New York Knicks, once said, "The athlete must eventually live all his days never able to recapture the feeling of those few years of intensified youth." Even now I can remember the feeling, but I can't duplicate it.

It has been said that athletes die twice. They lose a part of themselves when their sports days end and, later on, they die the real death.

No wonder some athletes fight the inevitable. "I'm never going to quit," declared Phil Simms, speaking of his quarter-backing career with the New York Giants. "They'll have to cut me. I won't make any graceful exits, absolutely not. You always hear about guys getting out while they're still on top, but how many do?... This is something I've wanted to do all my life and I can only do it for a certain short part of my life. I'm going to hang on as long as I can."

Adjusting to the end—learning to move beyond the game and go on with your life—is not easy, whether you're a professional athlete, a college athlete, or a high school athlete. A former baseball player talked about the temptation of returning to the sport when the Senior League started up. "It stirred up some good feelings, and it almost made me forget who I am now—a former pitcher, not an active one. The desire to get out there and play will always be in my blood, and I know I'll be tempted to dig up the spikes and glove again. As my off-season progresses, though, I'll need to understand that craving something doesn't necessarily mean it's good for me."

Adjusting to the end means adjusting, in most cases, to the quiet of a life without spectators and without applause. Adjusting to a new game, with new rules. It means growing up. Most of all, it means learning to live with feelings that may never, ever go away.

## Practice Time

• Identify which stage of athletic success you are currently in (if any).

• If you are in Stage Two (Dedication), think of ways you can develop other interests  as well as work on your sports. Possible suggestions:

  - I will read one book a month on a subject outside of athletics.
  - I work on developing friendships with people who are not involved in athletics.
  - I will participate in a least one non-athletic activity per month (i.e., attending a workshop, lecture, play, or concert).

• If you are in Stage Four (Extra Innings), try to understand the reasons behind why  you're hanging on to a career that's basically over.  Begin taking steps to make the break.  For example, seek career counseling, put together a résumé, set up some networking appointments, etc.

• Try to imagine your life without sports and evaluate how happy you are with it.  Focus on other things you value (relationships, education, jobs) and work to improve the quality of each.

• Try to apply the dedication and focus you commit to athletics to other aspects of your life and see how it can improve those aspects.

# PART TWO
## During the Game:
## Learning From the Sports Experience

# INTRODUCTION
# Life Lessons Learned from the Playing Field

*Since I never planned to live my life as an athlete, as a professional, I set my sights at Princeton on getting the best education I could. Anything else was a bonus. But football gave me values that were essential to a career in business: How to handle losses as well as wins. How to commit yourself to a goal...with dedication and discipline and the recognition of something bigger and deeper than one's self.*

-Dick Kazmaier, 1951 Heisman Trophy winner

*It doesn't matter if you win or lose—it's where you go after the game.*

-Television advertisement for McDonald's

I was having coffee with a friend of mine one morning when we got on the subject of whether sports really contribute to life. Without pause, my friend told me about a major turning point in his youth. Growing up in a small town in Pennsylvania, he had the good fortune of being a local athletic star. He won numerous wrestling championships at the league and state level. Then he started hanging around with a bad crowd—a crowd that ditched classes, hung out at the pool hall, and drank a lot of beer ("This was before drugs," he said). Then one day my friend's wrestling coach took him aside.

"That crowd will be doing the same things in 20 years," his coach stated. "Only, they'll be sneaking off from work instead of school, and drinking hard liquor instead of beer. You can be one of them, or you can continue to follow the path your sports experience has set in motion. It's your choice." My friend thought about it for some time. Finally, he chose to learn from the positive lessons sports taught him.

The late Arthur Ashe, who embodied all that was good about the athletic world, felt that sports are very important to young people—especially to:

the most vulnerable group in American life, 13-year-old black boys. With sports they are part of a team, they connect effort and reward, they accept fair play, they deal with losing. Too many of them associate losing with failure and embarrassment, and embarrassment in front of their peers is what leads young African-American men to get out their knives.

Sports are important not only for what they teach us, but for what they give us. One night my wife and I were invited by some dear friends to watch their daughter play junior varsity basketball. We ended up staying for the varsity game, as well. It was a well-played, two-point contest, but who won didn't really matter to me. What caught my attention was the play of the visiting team's point guard. She reminded me of what the sports experience can be—uplifting, beautiful—an example of the potential that lies in each human being. Her competency, her style, her spirit, and her intelligence on the court were pure poetry—more enjoyable and more inspiring than any movie or play I've seen in years.

Sports are often used as a metaphor for life because of the many valuable life lessons they can teach us. Sometimes, however, those lessons need to be pointed out before athletes can make the connection and profit from the sports experience.

Sports provide significant tools and lessons to assist on the path to success in the real world. If you learn what sports can teach, you won't walk onto the playing fields of life empty-handed.

As you read the next several chapters, think about the lessons of sports and how they apply to the world beyond sports. You might be surprised at just how much you can learn from your athletic experience.

# 3
# GETTING THE BIG PICTURE

## The Game Plan

In this chapter I will talk about:

- what it means to "get the big picture"
- why getting the big picture is important
- how getting the big picture can help you:
  - be a more complete person
  - make decisions about your future
- how sports can help you develop the ability to get the big picture

*If you don't know where you are going, you're sure to end up somewhere else.*
> *- Yogi Berra*

*Where there is no vision, the people perish...*
> *- Proverbs 29:18*

*Sometimes it strikes you as a football player that you have no other purpose in life but to go out there and hit people and make people go "Yay!" or "Boo." I think God put me on this planet to do more than that.*
> *- Ray Horton, Dallas Cowboy*

*I realized that if I wanted to keep traveling first class, I'd better plan ahead.*
> *- Frank Taveras, former Pittsburgh Pirate*

Quarterbacks know about getting the big picture. When they drop back from the line of scrimmage after the ball is snapped, they must see the whole field in a matter of seconds. They need to know who's open, who's double-teamed, and who's breaking through the line. They must determine whether it will be better to go for a short gain or a long one. Then they need to decide the best way to gain the required yardage. In the game of life, you'll get a lot farther by playing like a quarterback.

Take Steve Young, for example. This 49ers quarterback has been a winner since his days as a hot college prospect at Brigham Young University. Despite all his success, he's never lost sight of the fact that one day he's going to have to walk off the playing field and into a different kind of life. To make sure he has something to walk to, Young has spent his off-season time attending law school. As he told one journalist, "I don't want to go looking for a job after football and when someone asks if I'm qualified, I say, 'No, but remember that game? Wasn't that throw pretty?' "

## The Big Picture? What's That?

What does it mean when people talk about "getting the big picture"? Here are some of the definitions I've come up with:

• being aware of what is going on in the world around you
• knowing what is and isn't important to your long-term happiness
• using this information to make decisions that will have a positive impact on your future

Getting the big picture helps you prepare for the inevitable changes that will take place in your life. It makes you aware of what's happening in the world outside of sports and gives you a view of yourself as being a success at something besides athletics.

"It's a matter of being a complete person. Once you look at yourself as a basketball player only, you lose track of your opportunities. I've studied success. In the last two years, I've had more conversations with CEOs than I have with athletes. It's part of seeing a vision. Some people don't see that—like some people couldn't see us winning back-to-back world championships."

The above words of wisdom come from former Detroit Piston

star, Isaiah Thomas, one of the more famous players for Detroit. What you may not know is that Thomas, while an active NBA player, was also a successful businessman who co-owned several businesses. He's just as comfortable holding his laptop computer as he is holding a basketball. Isaiah Thomas has the big picture.

A lot of kids with dreams of becoming professional athletes don't look any further than that. But even if you are lucky (and talented) enough to become a professional athlete, your vision shouldn't stop there. "I would estimate that only five out of 100 athletes will not have to work again after they retire," says Brian Dowling, a former Yale star and professional football player who is developing a program to help athletes make the transition from sports to business.

As Doug Allen, assistant executive director of the NFL Players Association, says, "This is the one industry where you have to begin out-placement the day you get there."

Even if you know your future doesn't lie in the world of professional athletics, chances are you haven't given much thought as to where it does lie. Too many of us just kind of fall into a career. What to do for a living is a decision that affects our entire future, but most of us (especially when we're young) give more thought to choosing a pair of shoes. We just don't have the big picture.

In 1970, Dr. Edward Banfield of Harvard University wrote a book called *The Unheavenly City*. In it, he talked about a study he conducted on success. He wanted to find out how and why some people became financially independent during the course of their working lifetimes. The major reason for success in life, he discovered, was an attitude he called "long time perspective." The most successful men and women in life took the future into consideration with every decision they made. In other words, they "got the big picture."

## Sports and the Big Picture

How can sports help you develop the ability to get the big picture? One way is through visualization. Visualization is a technique with which many athletes are very familiar. It involves seeing yourself being successful at something. You may visualize yourself hitting a home run, clearing a hurdle, or making a perfect dismount. Now take that same visualization technique and make it work for you *outside of sports*. *See* yourself doing well on a test, making a speech, or being confident in a job interview. *See* yourself 5, 10, or 20 years from now. What are you doing? What do you want to be doing? What will it take to get there from here?

Sometimes sports can help you get the big picture in a roundabout way. "Shoulder surgery was a reality check for me. All of a sudden, USC saw a better student, a better all-round person who was looking for a future that did not include baseball," commented Casey Burrill, one-time University of Southern California baseball catcher.

Bill Bradley received scholarship offers from 75 schools. He finally turned down a full athletic scholarship at Duke University—a school with a nationally-renowned basketball team—to attend Princeton, a school where athletes had to pay their way. He chose Princeton because he decided it would be the best school for him as a student, not as an athlete. After all, what if he got injured and was no longer able to play basketball? Soon after that, Bradley did get hurt. Fortunately, it was only a minor foot injury, but it made him all the more sure about his decision to attend Princeton. It helped him focus on the big picture of where he ultimately wanted to go in life.

Some people might argue that sports prevent athletes from getting the big picture—that the time, energy, and focus that sports demand keep athletes from thinking about much else. That can certainly be true (see "Tunnel Vision" in the upcoming section). Still, I believe that the lesson is there for athletes who want to learn it.

Ultimately, success comes most readily to the athletes prepared for life outside of sports—those who have seen the big picture and realize the glory won't last forever.

## Practice Time

By now you should know why it's important to get the big picture. You should also know that sports can help you develop this ability. Hopefully, you're excited about putting what you've learned into practice. Here are some exercises that will help you:

### Seeing the Field #1
Strengthen your ability to "see the field." Do this by making a habit of reading the newspaper (the whole newspaper, not just the sports section) or listening to the news several times a week. Ask yourself how what you're reading or hearing might affect you.

### Seeing the Field #2
This is a little more specific than Exercise #1. Your goal is to learn more about the various career options that are available to you. This may involve talking to guidance or personal counselors, researching different jobs at the library, or talking to individuals who perform those jobs. Be creative. After all, there's a world of possibilities just waiting for you.

# 4
# HARD WORK
## Paying the Price for Success

### The Game Plan

In this chapter, I will talk about:

- what sports teach about hard work
- the Three D's of hard work: desire, determination, and discipline
- why hard work doesn't always guarantee success
- what hard work can teach you about life

*Let me tell you the secret that has led me to my goal. My strength lies solely in my tenacity.*
- Louis Pasteur

*To do a sport at a high level teaches you how to live. You just can't say, "It's a bad day." You have to work hard.*
- Tore Meinecke, former top-ranked tennis player, commenting on his rehabilitation after a serious car crash

Todd Williams, a top distance runner, discovered the value of hard work in college. At first, he thought because he had been a big-time jock in high school, he could do a little coasting. He soon learned otherwise. "I went from being this guy who never got beat to getting my butt kicked on the track every day. I wasn't serious about running. Three or four nights a week I'd go out drinking with the boys. I wasn't a crazy alcoholic, pot-smoking type of guy, but I lost control of things. I'd do all the workouts, but without putting in the work." He coasted in the classroom, too. On academic probation through his sophomore year, Williams came close to losing his athletic eligibility.

As his college coach said, "Todd always wanted to be the

best, but he thought he could party with the boys and still get to that level. There's no way you can do that. He went from being a good runner to a great runner because he decided —finally—to make some sacrifices."

That's what sports teach you: that natural ability helps, but it's not enough. You must be willing to pay the price if you want to succeed and that price is hard work.

## Triple Threat: Desire, Determination, and Discipline

People willing to work hard to get what they want usually possess three powerful traits: Desire, determination, and discipline.

### Desire: The Fire in the Belly

Desire is your constant companion during your playing days. It's what drives you to your best. This burning desire to succeed (Lee Iacocca called it the "fire in the belly") comes from within.

If your desire is strong enough, it breeds commitment—another essential quality for athletes. Mary Lou Retton wasn't your typical gymnast. Built more like a sprinter than a ballerina, she, nonetheless, had tremendous desire and committed herself to do the work necessary to reach her goal. A few weeks before the Olympics, Mary Lou required knee surgery. Less than 10 days later, she was back in the gym, performing a full workout. Her commitment and desire paid off with a gold medal.

Desire doesn't always come easy to athletes. Sometimes just keeping your desire burning is work. Pro golfer Curtis Strange won his second U.S. Open in 1989 and was recognized as the No.1 golfer in the world. Three years later, he had yet to win another tournament. What happened? He lost the desire to practice and prepare. As another top player put it, "After you've accomplished so much, sometimes it's tough to get out on the practice range; to spend that extra 30 minutes on the putting green. Deep down, you're pretty satisfied with yourself, and that's when problems start."

You've seen how important desire is to sports success. It's equally important to life outside of sports. Perhaps, even *more* important. Why? Because in the real world, there are no cheering crowds to get your adrenaline flowing. You have to do it yourself. The commitment to stay with an assignment—whatever it takes—until it's completed can only come from within you.

### Determination: The Ability to Keep on Going

Who can forget watching the women's marathon in the 1984 Olympics? Seeing that one, solitary runner stagger into the arena after everyone else had finished? Every step looked excruciatingly painful. The world held its collective breath, waiting for her to collapse, praying she wouldn't. I'm sure that desire had long left this woman, but determination hadn't. She was determined to finish the course, and she did.

Both in and out of the athletic world, determination is what keeps you moving forward when desire falters.

Lee Trevino is the all-time money winner in the history of professional golf. Desire played a big part in his success, but so did determination. As he says in Doris Lee McCoy's book, *Megatraits*:

> People often tell me, "You're the luckiest guy in the world. I wish I could do what you do." Well, they don't realize it, but they probably could. But you've got to be willing to sacrifice, whether it's as a computer operator or a professional golfer. You have to devote every spare moment to the field you've chosen. Of course, that means there are lots of things you're not going to be able to do, and some of those things might be things you enjoy. Maybe you won't be able to go away on weekends, or go camping or water skiing or whatever. In golf, there are a lot of players with potential, but they won't sacrifice for their goal. They'd rather quit practicing at 2:00 P.M. in the afternoon and go have a beer with the gang.

There will be times when desire leaves you. Maybe you're taking a required class that you really don't enjoy. Perhaps you're experiencing problems in a relationship and you're tired of trying to work things out. Or maybe you've been given an assignment by your boss that doesn't appeal to you. Your lack of desire may make you want to give up—flunk the class, walk out on the relationship, or do a poor job on your work assignment. But if you draw on the determination you learned as an athlete, you will work past your lack of desire. You'll do what needs to be done, even when you feel like doing something, anything, else.

### Discipline: Practice Makes Perfect

With desire and determination goes discipline. Rare is the athlete who makes it without discipline. Discipline gets you out of bed on a cold, rainy morning to run 10 or 20 miles or pushes you into a swimming pool to put in two hours of laps before school. It takes discipline to invest the days, weeks, and years of practice required to sustain a few hours of quality playing time.

Bill Bradley had that kind of discipline. "Growing up, I would practice several hours after school each day, and longer on the weekends. If someone asked why I pushed so hard, I would repeat a phrase from a favorite coach who used to say, 'When you're not practicing, someone somewhere is, and when you meet, given roughly equal ability, he will win.' I never wanted to lose because I had failed to make the maximum effort. I always wanted to be prepared, so I practiced."

If you've learned how to be disciplined as an athlete, then you've learned more than just how to develop your physical skills. You've also learned how to develop your mental skills. For example, discipline is a good tool for helping you solve problems. The disciplined person accepts responsibility for a problem; takes the time to analyze it and determine the best solution; and postpones the more immediate pleasure of ignoring a problem for the more long-term pleasure of conquering it as it arises.

Sometimes, however, athletes have a hard time being as disciplined off the field as they are on. I know that in my own athletic career discipline was no problem. I did whatever it took to improve. Transferring that discipline to the real world was harder. Like most people, I struggle to maintain a healthy diet and to exercise regularly, even though I realize these things are vital to my physical well-being.

The challenge is to understand that the discipline producing such satisfying results, athletically, can produce equally satisfying results in the real world. Dr. Bobby Brown, cardiologist and former president of the American League, is a good example of this.

He became a doctor while playing third base for the New York Yankees from 1946-1954. While his teammate, Yogi Berra, read comic books as they traveled from game to game, Brown read medical texts. Brown applied the same discipline he learned as a student-athlete in high school and college to balance life as a medical student and a professional baseball player. He had the desire, the determination, and the discipline to make it.

## The Hard Work Lesson

Hard work does not automatically equal success. Joe Montana worked hard to overcome the injuries that kept him off the football field for over two years, only to see his starting quarterback spot awarded to Steve Young. Hard work (and four Super Bowl rings) didn't get Joe what he wanted.

Nor is Joe alone. Every year, thousands of athletes, young and older, work and sweat and give it all they've got, only to find out they didn't make the team.

Dr. Julian Slowinski, a psychologist, former Benedictine monk, and high school coach, says: "I...believe the discipline of sports can be carried over into other fields. But, on the negative side, sports teaches you there is nothing you can't do if you work hard enough. In the corporate world, it's not always the hardest worker who gets ahead. I know a former high school star who still believes his coach was right in telling him you always win if you want it bad enough."

Does this mean you shouldn't bother working for what you want? No way. Sometimes work is important, not so much for what it *gets* you, as for what it *teaches* you. As a young coach, Jimmy Valvano once had a group of players ask him why winning was so important to him. "Because the final score defines you," he said. "You lose; ergo, you're a loser. You win; ergo, you're a winner."

"No," the players insisted. "The participation is what matters, the constancy of effort. Trying your very best, regardless of whether you win or lose—that's what defines you." It took another two decades before the lesson sunk in.

"They were right," Valvano told a writer. "The kids at Johns Hopkins were *right*. It's effort, not result. It's *trying*. God, what a great human being I could've been if I'd had this awareness back then."

Working hard does not always guarantee getting what you want. On the other hand, hard work *will* equal positive results. I've observed this first-hand on the playing field, in the counselor's office, and in the business suite.

There are no shortcuts to success. A lot of talented people never accomplish much because they're unwilling to pay the price. There are also a lot of people who aren't blessed with natural ability, but who succeed because they work harder than anyone else. When I played basketball, I always feared someone would take my spot in the starting lineup. After all, I was quite small. There was always someone bigger than me. But it never happened. Why? A big part of it was hard work. I simply tried harder than the rest.

In the long run, success in the real world is not reserved solely for those with the highest IQ's, the most talent, or the best physical appearance. Success outside of sports, like success in sports, comes to those who are willing to work for it.

## Practice Time

You know the value of hard work; you've seen what it can do for you as an athlete. Now it's time to make the Three D's of Hard Work—Desire, Determination, and Discipline—work for you in the real world.

### *Muscle Builder #1*
Pick a short-range goal. Some examples of short-range goals might be:

• I want to get a B+ or better on my next math test.
• I want to start a regular exercise program.
• I want to set up 10 job interviews this month.

Tell yourself how much you *desire* to achieve this goal. Using the *determination* and *discipline* that you learned as an athlete work towards completing this goal. (You may want to read the section on "Going for the Gold: Setting and Achieving Goals" before completing this exercise.)

### *Muscle Builder #2*
Pick a long-range goal. This involves asking yourself what you really want to achieve in life and whether you're willing to work and sacrifice to do it. Don't let yourself be swayed from doing something you *really want to do*. For example, a retired professional athlete might secretly want to be a doctor or lawyer, but talk him or herself out of it by saying, "By the time I finished school, I'd be a 40-year-old doctor just starting out." So what? You're going to turn 40, anyway, so you might as well turn 40 doing something you really want to do. Now, follow the instructions on achieving goals given above.

Try to spend one month, a week, or a day (depending on your time) being disciplined toward achieving one goal. Set your goal (make sure it's realistic) and apply the 3-D's toward realizing it.

# 5
# THE STUDENT ATHLETE
## How Sports Teach You to Learn

### The Game Plan

In this chapter, I will talk about:

- what learning skills that sports can teach you
- the traits of a good learner
- what the fundamentals of learning are
- why athletes are often thought of as "dumb jocks"

*It's what you learn after you know it all that counts.*
- John Wooden

*If you can take a round ball and bounce it on a flat surface and shoot it at a right angle and bounce it off a rectangular backboard and through an oval hoop, then you can learn algebra, you can learn geometry.*
- Joe Clark, former principal of East Side High School in Paterson, New Jersey, whose unorthodox approach to education was profiled in the film, *Lean on Me*

Having breakfast one day with John Dunning, University of Pacific women's volleyball coach and then president of the American Volleyball Coaches' Association, he made a rather interesting statement. "You know, George," he said, "when it comes to learning real life skills, sports is a better teacher than the classroom." He went on to explain: "First of all, kids who are seriously involved in athletics spend more time on the field than they do in the classroom, so there is simply more opportunity to learn. Second, the sports setting is more real-world oriented than the classroom. Kids have to take more risks; there are more demands placed on the skills they learn. In the classroom, you can coast. Do that on the playing field, and you won't last long."

John confirmed what I have long suspected—a person who

can "learn" a sport, can learn other things as well. In its own way, sports can help teach you anything from such fundamentals as algebra and geometry to life skills like goal-setting and risk-taking.

## The Traits of a Good Learner

You must be a good learner to excel in your sport. Your sports participation teaches you to *study* your performance and *learn* your weaknesses and strengths. You make adjustments and correct mistakes based on what you learn. In other words, if you get something wrong, you *practice* and *understand* the principles involved to avoid future errors.

As a player, always eager to learn more about the game, my teammates, my opponents, and myself, my curiosity to find a more effective way to "get it done" on the basketball court was insatiable.

Curiosity, openness, and a willingness to see things differently are the traits of a good athlete. And they are, universally, the earmarks of a good learner.

## The Fundamentals of Learning

John Wooden was one of college basketball's greatest coaches. Players dreamed of becoming part of his Bruin dynasty. But instead of learning exotic defenses and clever offensive patterns, Wooden's players spent most of their time drilling the (boring) fundamentals of basketball. Some, at times, resisted practicing what they already did well. Wooden's emphasis on the basics, however, paid off with 10 NCAA titles.

Good learners in school practice the fundamentals until they are as second-nature to them as dribbling is to a top basketball player. These fundamentals we all know from childhood as the "Three R's": Reading, wRiting, and aRithmetic. Mastering them is key to achieving a successful future in the world beyond sports. It can be hard. Worse, it can be boring. Few enjoy learning sentence structure. And drilling the basics of good grammar can be as pleasant as a trip to the dentist. But before you can write a bestselling novel, knowing those basic things is essential.

In life, as in sports, mastering the fundamentals is the challenge. How successful you become literally depends on how well you make the basics a part of you. It is the foundation upon which your achievements will be built. Michael Jordan worked hard as a kid just to be an average player. Jordan met the challenge. And from that solid base, soared to the very top of the basketball world.

## Overcoming the "Dumb Jock" Stereotype

A lot of people feel that sports and intelligence do not exactly go hand-in-hand. Is the "dumb jock" stereotype just that—something that actually applies to only a small percentage of the athletic population? Or is there more truth to it?

I think it's safe to say that the majority of high school, college, and professional athletes are not stupid. Nevertheless, athletes sometimes fall prey to certain learning barriers that leave them ill-prepared to face the intellectual challenges of life beyond sports. These barriers include:

### Passivity (The "Let-Someone-Else-Do-It" Syndrome)
In some cases, the passivity enforced by years of someone else making your decisions leads you to make poor decisions when no one's around to help get you through life's everyday challenges. We humans are creatures of habit and many athletes get into the habit of letting others take charge of their lives.

Not all jocks fall victim to this. Fred Brown, who played basketball for Georgetown University, realized that his chances of making it to the pros were slim. He decided to use his athletic ability as a different kind of stepping stone to success. Combining his sociology degree and his sports contacts, he developed a million-dollar business in marketing and real estate investment. He then went on to attend Georgetown Law School.

Bob Shannon has coached football for nearly 20 years at East St. Louis High School in a poor, crime-ridden community. Yet Shannon's teams have won six state championships, and, more importantly, his athletes maintain a grade-point average higher than the rest of the school.

Shannon sees football—everything from blocking schemes to what plays to call in certain situations—as training for making the right choices. One of the choices his athletes are responsible for is their own education.

## Poor Education

In other cases, the lack of a quality education blocks the path. This is especially true in the case of inner-city athletes. As Wayne Embry, general manager of the Cleveland Cavaliers, stated, "Quite often, coming out of school, these kids don't know anything else but basketball. Someone's altered their test scores to get them into school, and once they're in, they're directed to take basketweaving and plays-and-games, or whatever the hell it is. Tell me what they're going to do in our society."

## Learning Disabilities

Sometimes people are perceived as "dumb" for other reasons. Russell White was an outstanding tailback at the University of California (Berkeley), ultimately becoming the school's number three all-time rusher. His career at Cal got off to a shaky start, however. He was admitted to the school as a Proposition 48 student due to his inability to score 700 on the SAT, despite several tries. The problem was later diagnosed as dyslexia, a learning disability. "At first, I thought I was just a big, stupid athlete," White said. "Learning I have dyslexia lifted a big weight and gave me a chance to breathe." With his problem finally diagnosed, White graduated from the university with a degree in social welfare.

## Ego, Etc.

Why do many athletes have such a hard time graduating from college? One answer may be in this excerpt from a *TIME* magazine article, which summarizes the academic experience of many college players:

> Like student athletes at many other schools, UNLV's players often arrive on campus with severe reading problems, poor study skills and swollen egos. They practice as much as four hours

a day, seven days a week, and miss 30 to 40 days of classes because of road games. During their absence, note takers are hired to attend classes for them. All players are required to attend a two-hour study hall after practice, but some are so exhausted they can barely keep their eyes open. UNLV's graduation rate is better than that of many schools, although only 40% of the team ever get degrees. It's an unrealistic expectation," says Diana Costello, head academic tutor for the team. If subjected to the same grueling workouts, she adds, even "the finest of students would have a difficult time."

There is evidence that administrators are beginning to realize the difficulties student-athletes face. The NCAA has restricted the number of hours athletes are allowed to practice. In many sports, the playing season has also been limited. The NCAA has voted to make freshmen ineligible for varsity sports beginning in 1996—a move that would hopefully reduce the pressure of trying to adjust to college and college sports at the same time.

Actions such as these will give athletes more time to focus on their academic careers. That still doesn't mean it will be easy to be a player *and* a scholar. Achieving success off the field means hurdling the barriers thrown in your path and showing the same eagerness to learn that you did on the field. Your sports training has given you the skills—you need only apply them to the larger world.

## Practice Time

You have many skills to help you be a good learner; now it's time to transfer them to real world situations.

### *Mastering the Fundamentals #1*
The average American adult reads less than one book per year. And 58 percent of the American population never reads another non-fiction book, cover to cover, upon finishing high school.

Ask a close friend to suggest his or her favorite subject. Then visit your local library or bookstore. Pick out a couple of books on the suggested subject and read the introductions. You'll be surprised at how this can expand your interests and reading skills.

### *Mastering the Fundamentals #2*
Unplug your TV for the day. Better yet, put it in the closet. Incredible as the idea may seem, you might find that the closet is just the right place for it. Now, what can you do with this quiet time to help your learning skills? You can:

- Read the newspaper (at least the front page of every section). This will help you stay on top of what's going on in the world.
- Read the editorial section of the newspaper or magazine. This tells you not only what's happening, but what people think about it.
- Start a journal. Keeping a journal helps your writing skills and helps you learn more about yourself.
- Study. Even if you're not in school, there are probably things you wish you knew more about. Get some books from the library and start learning.

# 6
# GOING FOR THE GOLD
## Setting and Achieving Goals

### The Game Plan

In this chapter I will talk about:

- what sports teach you about goals
- why setting goals is important to success
- common mistakes people make when setting goals
- tips for setting *and achieving* your goals

*No matter what the competition or what the training, I've always tried to find a goal and better it.*
> - Bonnie Blair, the most decorated U.S. Olympian, with five gold medals and six overall

*I know one day all the phone calls will stop. Basketball will be over. That's why I've set such academic goals for myself.*
> - Randy Livingstone, a high school basketball player at Isodore Newman School in New Orleans, Louisiana

When hockey star Mario Lemieux was diagnosed with Hodgkin's disease, he received some words of advice from another Hodgkin's survivor—former Olympian Jeff Blatnick.

"As athletes, we're goal-oriented. It might be good for Mario to be thinking about playing again six to eight weeks from now because that creates a challenge for him. He can become pro-active instead of passive in his recovery."

Goals should be familiar to anyone who has participated in athletics as everything about athletics is goal-oriented. The most significant aspects of sports are setting, striving for, and achieving goals. This is also true in life.

Successful athletes set goals to get more first serves in play, block more shots, catch more passes, raise their shooting percentage, or to improve their personal bests.

I started setting goals as a seven- or eight-year-old on a playground basketball court. I spent hours playing imaginary basketball games while carefully recording the number of shots it took to reach 50 points and victory for my team.

As I got older, I wrote down my goals before each game and reviewed them a few minutes before tip-off. This ritual always helped me focus on the contest and measure my effectiveness.

Goal setting is a "sports tool" that will prove invaluable to your success after sports. Its sole purpose is to assist you in accomplishing what you want. Setting, planning, and working towards goals lead to the victory stand in life after sports.

## Setting Goals: Saying Yes to Your Dreams

*People don't like to set goals, because they don't like to fail. But we get tougher by setting goals. You've got to push the envelope to find out how far you can go.*

- Jim Loehr, sports psychologist and co-owner of LGE Saddlebrook
Sports Science

Athletes know how important setting goals is to achieving athletic success. However, you may not realize why setting goals is important to success in the real world.

A study conducted at Yale University in 1953 found that only three percent of that year's graduates had set specific career goals. Twenty years later, in 1973, that three percent proved wealthier and had accomplished more than the other 97 percent combined. In the absence of clearly defined goals, people spin their wheels at busy work.

Goals crystallize thought and provoke action. They keep you focused on what's important and aid your decision-making. You are in better control of your life as well. Setting goals is the key to performing at your peak.

Finally, obtaining your goals creates a sense of satisfaction, pride, and confidence in yourself.

## Common Goal-Setting Mistakes

Just setting goals, however, doesn't guarantee that you will achieve them. Saying to yourself, "I want to lose 20 pounds this year," and then going about life as usual will not make you 20 pounds lighter. You must develop or find strategies for losing weight, decide which is best for you, and then implement your weight-loss plan.

In his bestselling book, _Psycho-Cybernetics_, Dr. Maxwell Maltz compares the goal-setting process to the homing system in a torpedo. Once the torpedo's target is set, the self-adjusting system constantly monitors feedback signals from the target area. Using the feedback data to adjust the course setting in its navigational computer, the torpedo makes the corrections necessary to stay on target. If programmed incompletely or non-specifically—or aimed at a target too far out of range—the torpedo erratically wanders around until its propulsion system fails or it self-destructs.

Here are some of the most common mistakes people make when setting goals:

- They don't say how they will measure their progress.
- The goals they set are really someone else's goals.
- They set goals that conflict with one another.
- They set too many goals.

Sometimes, people focus too much on their vision of what they want, and not enough on the work necessary to achieve that vision. I was reminded of this one afternoon a few years ago when I wandered into the Stanford gym to watch basketball practice. A young man practiced shot after shot from the free throw line. I recognized him as a player who had shot less than 40 percent from the line the two previous seasons. His coach, who knew I was a psychologist, commented to me: "You'll be happy to know we just sent [the player] to a sports psychologist to work on his mental approach to shooting free throws, and we think he's going to be vastly improved."

Interested, I watched the young man continue his practice. Then I noticed he had a terrible hitch in his shot. I thought, the kid's mind wasn't what needed work; it was his shooting form. By moving his hand forward six inches when he got set to start his shot, the young man could eliminate the hitch and greatly improve his chances of making the shots—and maybe even get his money back from the sports psychologist!

## Tips for Setting and Achieving Goals

The hardest part in accomplishing any goal is getting started. Remember the Law of Inertia from your physics class? A body at rest tends to stay at rest. Fortunately, the converse is also true; a body in motion tends to stay in motion. So start with small steps that you know you can do. The momentum will keep you going.

Here are some other ways to make the goal-setting process work for you:

**Effective Goal-Setting**
- *Write down your goals.*
  Written goals become self-fulfilling prophecies.
- *Be positive.*
  State what you want to *do*. If you want to stop doing something, state your goal in terms of what you want to do instead.
- *Make your goals measurable.*
  The more specific and measurable your goals are, the easier they will be to achieve.

You make a goal measurable by setting objectives. An objective is a milestone in a plan for accomplishing a goal. It's a measure of accomplishment. Remember the weight-loss example? Having a goal without objectives is like planning to lose weight by saying, "I'll start losing weight on January 1st, and by September 1st, I will have lost 20 pounds." Each objective is a planned stop along the path toward your goal. In this case, your objective might look like this:

- I will exercise three times a week for 30 minutes each time.
- I will limit myself to one dessert per week.
- I will try to lose two pounds per month.

**Make your goals obtainable.**
I hate exercise. Well, not really, but it doesn't make my Top 10 list of enjoyable things to do. Sports competition was pure

enjoyment for me; exercise for health's sake is 180 degrees different.

When I start thinking things like, "I have to exercise for the rest of my life if I'm going to maintain my health," I get really discouraged.

So I break it into steps that give me some immediate reward. I don't think in terms of exercising for the rest of my life; I think in terms of "five more minutes on the treadmill," or "three more laps in the pool."

## Always keep your goals in sight.

Florence Chadwick was the first woman to swim the English Channel. The first time she tried she failed, even though she was just a few miles from the shore. Her problem? Heavy fog and choppy water prevented her from seeing the goal. The next time she tried, she held a mental picture of the coastline in her head at all times. This time, the fog did not deter her because even when she couldn't physically see her goal, she could see it mentally. She kept her goal in "sight" until she finally achieved it.

## Make the process enjoyable.

Lastly, perhaps the most important step in obtaining your goals is to make the process fun. If you don't enjoy the journey, then the goal itself will be robbed of much of its sweetness.

## Practice Time

Think of three things you would like to achieve during the next month. Select one and, using the goal-setting guidelines you just read, write a one-month action plan. This action plan should include:

- a list of what you will need to accomplish your goal
- a list of the qualities and resources you already have that will help you accomplish your goal
- specific objectives that will help you accomplish your goal

Make a list of four things you will do this week that will get you started on achieving your goal. Put a reminder of what you need to do to achieve your goal where you can see it many times a day. A bathroom mirror, dresser drawer, or briefcase may be good places.

# 7
# PULLING TOGETHER
## The Importance of Teamwork

### The Game Plan

In this chapter I will talk about:

* why teamwork is becoming increasingly important in the world outside sports
* the positive and negative aspects of teamwork
* how teamwork can help you develop satisfying personal relationships

*A football team is like a fine watch—all precisioned. If one small part is not working in harmony, the watch fails to function properly.*
- Knute Rockne

One of the most powerful lessons from the playing field is that no one wins alone. When Wesley Theodore Englehorn, a tackle at Dartmouth who was a Walter Camp All-America pick in 1912, celebrated his 103rd birthday, he remembered football best, especially, "The teammates. The teamwork. One man can't do it by himself."

Even in an individual sport, parents, coaches, and others provide support along the way. They are part of your team.

Teamwork is as important off the field as it is on. The models for today's business environment are participative management, collaboration, self-directed work groups, and cooperation. These are simply other ways of saying teamwork. I spend a considerable amount of time each week with presidents of organizations all asking the same question, "How can I get my people to perform better?" These leaders understand that the success or failure of their organizations has a lot to do with how their "teams" work.

Society is a complex web of interdependent groups and teams.

People are called on to work with each other in their professions, at home, in school, and in other organizations. Your athletic experience should prepare you well to play a significant role on these teams.

For example, Sen. Bill Bradley found that the elements of being part of a basketball team—working together, agreeing on a common goal, sharing the credit—are the same ones he employs as a legislator. You, too, will discover that the teamwork skills you develop as an athlete will serve you well in other walks of life.

## The Ups and Downs of Teamwork

If you ask parents what they want their children to learn from playing sports, almost all would probably say, "Teamwork." Ideally, a child or youth who participates on sports teams learns such valuable lessons as how to cooperate with others, how to play a needed role rather than be the star, and how to play fairly.

Unfortunately, some team situations are less than ideal. Sometimes teamwork consists more of competition than cooperation. Team members compete among themselves for rewards, recognition, or playing time.

A recent example of this is the Steve Young/Joe Montana quarterback controversy in the early '90s. Both players wanted to be the San Francisco 49ers' starter. Their intense competition was rarely beneficial for the team. I think Joe Montana recognized that when he was finally traded to the Kansas City Chiefs. He commented that one reason he was happy about the trade was because he realized the San Francisco players had made the transition to Young, and he didn't want to disrupt that.

There are many fields where teamwork is critical—fields where lives are at stake, not points. I'm thinking of surgical teams, SWAT teams, firefighters. On these teams, as well as on others, sometimes one person is in the lead, then another. Roles change. To obtain the goal, you sometimes have to accept a lesser role.

I was a point guard in college. Sometimes my role was to be a scorer, to put the ball up and get our team some much needed points. At other times, my role was more focused on passing the ball and making sure everyone was involved in the game. Still other times my job became to make sure the younger players got easy shots early to build their confidence for the rest of the game.

I learned early in my youth to contribute in whatever way necessary to give us the best chance of winning. As a team player, my contribution was determined by how it impacted the final result. If I did my part but we lost, I never felt that wonderful. If I did my part and we won, that was special. That lesson has guided me in all aspects of my life. It is perhaps the greatest lesson I learned in sports.

## Teammates and Friendships

*Friendships forge a bond on our team and create a situation where the whole is greater than the sum of its parts. Nothing can match the sense of fulfillment of being surrounded by people who care for you as you work together to achieve a goal.*
- Debbie Hill, head volleyball coach at the College of William and Mary.

One advantage to being a member of a team is that it gives you the opportunity to develop rich and satisfying friendships. You should learn to truly enjoy the intimate relationships you can establish through sports. Each teammate (or opponent) shouldn't be viewed as a threat to your own sense of self-worth.

Unfortunately, many athletes (especially males) seldom develop true intimacy with their teammates, let alone their opponents.

Sometimes competition gets in the way. In junior high school my best friend and I played sports every day. We were inseparable. But our relationship was always limited by the barrier of the intensity of our competition. It was a real love/hate relationship and we had the fights to prove it.

Later, as a shy, insecure young man in college, I totally failed to take the time to enjoy and benefit from the opportunities I had to get to know my teammates off the court. It is a loss that I regret to this day.

When I think of an example of someone who used sports to

establish deep friendships, I think of Magic Johnson. When he was diagnosed with the HIV virus, who were some of the people he called? Teammates like Kareem, and opponents like Larry Bird and Isaiah Thomas. These were the people he knew he could count on.

## Practice Time

Like everything else, teamwork skills require constant practice in order to make them sharp. Here are two exercises you might want to try:

### Pulling Together #1
Look for opportunities to exercise your teamwork skills by joining a school club, community group, or some other type of organization that interests you. Volunteer to be a part of an action committee. Commit yourself to helping your "team" achieve its goal.

### Pulling Together #2
Make an effort to develop a friendship with a teammate or former teammate. (It might be helpful to use the goal-setting guidelines learned in the last section.)

# 8

# IMPROVING YOUR HANDICAP
## Eliminating the Mistakes in Your Game

### The Game Plan

In this chapter I will talk about:

- how sports teach you to overcome and eliminate mistakes
- not letting your mistakes get the best of you
- how you can forgive yourself (and others) and get on with the job

In the 1993 NCAA championship game between Michigan and North Carolina, Michigan lost after player Chris Webber called a non-existent time-out during the last seconds of the game. Among the hundreds of letters Webber received after his error was this handwritten one from Washington, D.C.:

Dear Chris:

I have been thinking of you a lot since I sat glued to the TV during the championship game.

I know that there may be nothing I or anyone can say to ease the pain and disappointment of what happened.

Still, for whatever it's worth, you, and your team, were terrific.

And part of playing for high stakes under great pressure is the constant risk of mental error.

I know. I have lost two political races and made countless mistakes over the last 20 years. What matters is the intensity, integrity and courage you bring to the effort. That is certainly what you have done.

You can always regret what occurred but don't let it get you down or take away the satisfaction of what you have accomplished.

You have a great future. Hang in there.

Sincerely,
Bill Clinton

Sports teach you a lot about overcoming and eliminating mistakes simply because they give you so many opportunities to make mistakes in the first place. A receiver drops a pass, a third baseman lets the ball go between his legs, a tennis player charges the net when she should have dropped back. Athletic competition is a high-pressure situation, and, as President Clinton noted, where there is pressure, there is greater chance of error.

There is also greater opportunity for learning. For example, you learn that one way to increase the pressure on yourself is to worry about the possibility of making a mistake. You learn that if you want to become a successful athlete, this is a trap that you must avoid. You learn that beating yourself up only brings more disappointing play. The better you feel about yourself, the better you perform. So you learn to build your confidence with positive "self-talk." You tell yourself you've caught hundreds of passes, fielded thousands of groundballs, and that you will continue to do so. This helps reduce the number of mistakes you do make.

In 18 years of coaching, I have always emphasized that you win games by reducing your errors. The same is true in the real world. Reducing and eliminating mistakes improves your performance whether it be on the job, in your relationships, or in other areas of your life.

One of the best examples I can think of when it comes to overcoming and eliminating mistakes is the late Arthur Ashe. As one writer stated: "Ashe was the best at leaving every shot behind. He played each stroke as if it were for life and death and then instantly abstained from regret or celebration because there was another shot to play. It was inefficient, even self-destructive to waste energy raging at himself or his opponent or the umpire, even though to do so is wholly human...Ashe's blithe shrugging off of errors and injustices seemed almost lackadaisical, as if he didn't care. Yet his was the truer picture of focus. He cut his losses and moved on, unharmed by them."

## Don't Let Mistakes Get the Best of You

You are going to make mistakes in life. Mistakes are part of the life game as well as the sports game. But you can't let your mistakes get you down. I learned this lesson playing shortstop in junior high school. If I made an error, I worried about it, hung my head, and sure enough—I'd make another error on the next fielding chance. I finally learned that once the play is over, it's over and the game starts anew. Mistakes are part of the game, but successful people don't let their mistakes get the best of them.

At 18, Chespi Serna was a guard on the state champion Brea-Olinda's varsity basketball squad, one of California's winningest girls' teams. She was also the mother of a four-month-old son. She admitted that having a child so young was a mistake, but was determined to make the best of it. Making the best of it meant juggling school, sports, and motherhood as well as becoming the first in her family to graduate from high school. It meant hope-fully going on to college and a career working with computers.

Sometimes we make one mistake and think we've blown the whole game. Seldom is that true. However, as Chespi Serna learned, correcting that mistake isn't always easy.

At one of the most stressful times in my life, I visited a thera-pist. There wasn't a whole lot he could tell me, other than live through the crisis. But he said something that helped, some-thing I have shared with countless others throughout the years. As I rose from the chair, the doctor said, "George, remember: One step at a time."

Sports teach you that you get back into the game by making one play at a time. Similarly, the best way to overcome your fumbles in life is by taking one step at a time.

## How to Forgive and Move On

*Everybody messes up in life, you know. As long as you realize your mistake, you'll be alright.*

- Lloyd Daniels, San Antonio Spurs player and recovering drug and alcohol addict

Part of overcoming a mistake involves forgiving yourself for making the mistake in the first place. That can be harder than it sounds.

I often wonder why there are so many sermons on forgiveness. It's probably because there's not enough of it in our lives. People aren't very good at forgiving themselves or others. Athletes learn that forgiveness is a habit that can be acquired.

Forgiveness starts with you. You learn how to forgive yourself and then you can forgive others.

A teammate in college taught me how to forgive myself on the basketball court. After missing a lay-up or throwing a bad pass, my teammate would immediately make a fist and pound it into his palm. Then he would continue playing, never indicating that his failure was still with him.

I have been participating in and witnessing athletic events all my life, but I continue to be impressed with the athletes I see who do not point a finger when a teammate makes an error or fails to perform. They don't have time to waste in blame; their goal is to overcome the setback and win.

So forgive yourself and get on with the job.

How do you forgive yourself? By:

- accepting yourself as a human being
- seeing mistakes as opportunities to grow and learn
- understanding that failure is part of life

I've observed that most people learn more from their mistakes than their victories. So while you strive for perfection in the things you do, you shouldn't be afraid of your mistakes, or of taking the risks that lead to them.

## Practice Time

### *Moving On #1*

Is there an area of your life where you're making a mistake (i.e.; smoking, drinking too much, not making an effort to do well in school, etc.)? Target one error you would like to overcome or a bad habit you would like to eliminate. Resolve to overcome this problem one step at a time. Set up a goal plan for doing so.

### *Moving On #2*

Sharpen your ability to forgive yourself and others. Think of a forgiveness "cue" (for example, snapping your fingers, shrugging your shoulders, pounding your fist into your hand). The next time you or someone else makes a mistake, snap your fingers (or whatever your forgiveness "cue" is) and resolve not to dwell on the mistake. Do this until it becomes a habit with you.

Try to forgive in your relationships. Try not to dwell on people's idiosyncrasies and focus on their positive aspects.

# 9

# FOURTH DOWN AND INCHES TO GO
## Taking the Risks That Count

## The Game Plan

In this chapter I will talk about:

- why achieving your goals involves taking risks
- what might keep you from taking risks
- how sports can improve your risk-taking ability
- the steps to successful risk-taking

*If you don't invest very much, then defeat doesn't hurt very much and winning is not very exciting.*
- Dick Vermeil, former NFL Coach

*Security is mostly superstition. It does not exist in nature, nor do children experience it. Life is either a learning adventure or nothing.*
- Helen Keller

Quite frankly, achieving your goals involves taking risks. I remember coaching a group of boys one summer in a basketball league. In one game, we were up against the perennial league champions. As the game came down to the closing seconds, the score was tied. Suddenly, one of our players was wide open for the potential winning shot. The kids on the bench yelled, "Shoot, Dave!" But instead of shooting, Dave passed the ball to a teammate. The other boy couldn't get the shot off and passed the ball right back to Dave. "Shoot, Dave! Shoot!" the bench shouted. Again, he passed the ball.

We lost in overtime.

After the game, Dave's father sought me out. "Is Dave a bad shot?" he asked.

"Not at all. He's a good shot," I replied.

"Then why...?"

I thought a moment and then said, "I guess he's just afraid he'll miss the basket."

Dave personified a problem that keeps many of us from succeeding—the fear of taking a shot at what we want. Taking risks is the single most important factor in any kind of growth and yet we hesitate. Why?

## What Keeps You From Taking Risks

*I have to work a little harder because I have limitations, but that's okay. I can accomplish anything I want to accomplish. And, as long as I try, I'm never a failure. The failure is not trying.*
- Ada Myers, two-time women's national amputee gold champion

*The only time you can't afford to fail is the last time you try.*
- Charles Kettering

One thing that stops us from taking risks is the fear of what others might think. For example, you might say to yourself: "I'm not going to try out for the school play. People will think I'm a geek."

Some people avoid risks because that's their personality. They prefer security over excitement; contentment over passion. They find rocking the boat only makes them seasick.

Low self-esteem keeps others away from risks. They're afraid they won't measure up. At the plate, they never swing; they're set up for the shot but pass instead.

Fear of failure is probably the number one reason why people shun risk-taking. No one likes not succeeding.

Athletes know more than they like about failure. What athlete hasn't fumbled the ball, missed a serve, or dropped the baton? Failure, though, is not the worst thing in the world. As Ada Myers said, the worst thing is not trying.

In almost every sports competition, someone loses. If athletes only competed when guaranteed a win, we wouldn't have much competition. If every athlete walked off the field after a mistake, never to return, we would have empty fields!

Every time you take a risk, you risk failure. Does that mean you should never take a risk? Of course not. Baseball's legendary Babe Ruth once said, "I just keep going up there and swingin' at 'em." That's all we need do. Even though you might strike out, keep stepping up to the plate and swinging.

Risk-takers know they make progress even when they fail. Mistakes are learning tools, not sticks with which to beat yourself.

## How Sports Improve Your Ability to Take Risks

Peak performers in all areas—sports, medicine, academia—willingly accept risks. Peak performers don't play it safe. In my consulting business, I've worked with many company leaders. These individuals reached the top due to their ability and willingness to take chances. They understand that risk-taking is at the heart of the American system of free enterprise—beginning with those first Pilgrims who risked everything to come to a new land and a new life.

As an athlete you learn to take risks. You learn to go for the attempted steal in baseball, the long bomb in football, the drop-shot in tennis. You dare to be a winner, even if it means risking defeat.

Athletics teach us (or should teach us) not to fear failure. A lot of people back off at the first sign of failure or potential defeat. They doubt themselves, hesitate, retreat. This is not the lesson of the playing field.

## Tips for Taking Risks Off the Field

Not all athletes are born risk-takers. Some learn. Similarly, you may have to learn how to take risks off the playing field. Here are some of the steps that successful risk-takers follow:

• *Plan ahead.*
Having flexible, long-term goals will help you determine the necessary risks to achieve them. And a smart risk-taker *always* has a backup plan.

• *Do your homework.*
Research every angle before you take a risk. Business leaders

know better than to jump at every risky proposition that comes along. After all, there are risks that make sense and others that don't. It would be, for instance, pretty risky for me to climb a 10-meter diving board and try to do a Greg Louganis imitation. It was risky enough for Greg Louganis. But the difference between Greg Louganis and me is that his diving was an educated, informed risk, whereas, mine would be sheer stupidity.

• *Always remain calm.*

Don't let yourself be swept away in emotion. Know that you are educated and be confident in your abilities.

• *Evaluate the consequences.*

You have to be prepared to lose and live with it. If you can't do that, then the risk is too big to take.

• *Consider the timing.*

The time might not be right to take chances. This is not to say it won't be right later.

• *Hang around other risks-takers.*

Their success stories will keep you going.

Remember, a good risk is never an act of desperation. In basketball, you set up that risky, game-winning shot by running down the clock, calling time-outs, and getting the ball to the right person to take the highest-percentage shot.

In the real world, successful risk-takers, likewise, continually try to improve their position so they will be in the best possible shape for the next risk. They don't try to win games with a final shot; but, if it comes down to the wire, they take the best shot possible.

## Practice Time

*Setting Up the Shot*

Following the steps to successful risk-taking, set yourself up to take a risk off the playing field. Here are some examples:

For the high school athlete:
- Try out for a part in the school play
- Try out for a position on the school newspaper
- Run for student government (athletic representative)

For the college athlete:
- Take a course that you were afraid might be too hard for you
- Set up an interview for a job or internship in a challenging field
- Talk to your professor about a class you are taking and ask him or her questions

For the professional athlete:
- Improve your money-management skills by starting an investment program
- Explore learning a new field with an eye toward off-season and post-season career employment

# 10
# DOWN BUT NOT OUT
## Bouncing Back From Adversity

### The Game Plan

In this chapter I will talk about:

- what sports teach you about adversity
- how sports can help you learn to deal with life's obstacles

*Being cut (from my high school team) definitely had a big effect on me. It was embarrassing...They posted the list in the locker room, and it was there for a long time without my name on it.*

*I was down about not making it for a while, and I thought about not playing anymore. Of course, I did keep on playing, and whenever I was working out and got tired and figured I ought to stop, I'd close my eyes and see that list in the locker room without my name on it, and that usually got me going again.*
                    *- Michael Jordan*

Ron Guidry, a pitcher with the New York Yankees, almost quit baseball when he was sent back down to the minors early in his career. The Yankee management told him that he just wasn't ready for the big leagues. Guidry took it hard. He went home and told his wife, "That's it. I'm not going back to the minors! I've worked like the dickens to get here. I've made it and I can't go back."

The Guidrys packed their belongings and started driving to the family home in the South. As they drove, Ron's wife tried to get him to accept going to the minors because she knew baseball was his first love. Not far from their destination, they stopped at a restaurant. In that restaurant, Guidry decided not to let this latest setback get the best of him.

**71**

"Okay," he said, "one more time. I'm going to give it one more chance." That "one more" try took Guidry to the career he had dreamed of.

## Sports: Lessons in Adversity

Sports are great for teaching about adversity. You learn about individual setbacks, team setbacks, and losing streaks. Sports offer first-hand looks at some of the obstacles life can put in front of you.

If you let them, these obstacles can easily throw you off track. Keith Millard's devastating 1990 knee injury was not the first obstacle the Minnesota Viking defensive tackle had faced. A troubled childhood led to an equally troubled adolescence, which reached its climax in his senior year of high school when his mother threw him out of the house. Millard also had problems with alcohol and an explosive temper. A brief stay at the Hazeldon Drug and Alcohol Treatment Center, along with intensive counseling, finally helped Millard gain more control over his life. As he said in a July 1991 issue of *Sports Illustrated*:

> Every lesson I've learned, I've had to learn the hard way. No matter what my destiny is, it's not a straight line. It's five steps straight ahead, then over the mountains, through the water, through the jungle and five steps ahead again. There are always major obstacles in my life. Maybe I'll fall down the stairs, but I'll get back up. I was put on this earth to survive.

Most of us grow up with the idea that life ought to "work out" all the time. We feel cheated or discouraged when it doesn't. What we fail to understand is that life isn't supposed to "work out." It's not designed that way. Sports can help us make sense of this concept.

In sports, we learn that we can't always win and, two, that winning usually doesn't come easy. It's a challenge. Life is a challenge, too. It requires work of us. We must face and overcome obstacles. Even then we still don't always win.

If anyone in the sports world had an obstacle to overcome, it was baseball pitcher Jim Abbott. Born without a right hand, Abbott, nonetheless, became a star pitcher at the University of Michigan and a No.1 draft choice for the California Angels. In addition, as a member of the 1988 U.S. Olympic team, he pitched an entire championship game. Things were hard for Abbott. As his dad said, "When he was growing up, there would be things said to him, kids giving him a rough time, but we'd just send him right back out the door. We would try to encourage him. Now he encourages us."

Setbacks and obstacles mark the real world. For eight years, a young man with a dream walked the streets of Southern California. He dreamed of designing and operating a new kind of family theme park. No one would be interested, everyone said. Families preferred to go on picnics and outings.

Over the years, banks and other financial institutions refused to back the young man. His family, friends, and business associates told him to give it up. He went through bankruptcy. His name? Walt Disney.

Sports teach you that setbacks can be painful, but most of them are merely momentary. Sports also allow you opportunities to develop qualities helpful in dealing with adversity. Let's examine some of these qualities.

## "Tools" for Adversity

*Sports toughened Cragun for a recent financial blow. A company Cragun bought was dragged into the previous owner's bankruptcy. Cragun lost the $50,000 he'd paid for the company.*

*"It was start-over time at age 48," he said, "but I'm back on top again. I attribute that to what I learned from football. It taught me that I didn't have to quit. If I kept trying, I could win. Just because you've got a pile of people on you doesn't mean it will always be that way. You'll always have another series of downs when you can carry the ball again."*

—"Fame is Fleeting," *Desert News*, July 28, 1991

One of the many advantages sports participation provides is the chance to develop those qualities, or "tools," that will help you face some of life's tougher blows. These tools are: Perseverance, courage, and experience.

### Perseverance

Perhaps the greatest lesson I learned from the late George "Shorty" Kellogg, my YMCA coach, is that when you get knocked down in a game, you get right back up.

Sports teach you not to give up. Remember that wild-card playoff game between the Buffalo Bills and the Houston Oilers? Houston was up by 32 points in the third quarter, Buffalo's two biggest stars—Jim Kelly and Thurman Thomas—were out of action. Even die-hard Bill fans were switching the channel. But did Buffalo give up? No. They came back and won the game.

As Roger Staubach said, "Life is all about the ability to deal with the tough times. I get down. I get discouraged. I get frustrated...but I won't give up. If you have enough perseverance, it is amazing what you can accomplish."

### Courage

To be an athlete takes courage. Whether diving off a high dive tower or meeting an opponent in the boxing ring, you must call upon your courage to perform. To push your body to the limits of what it can achieve—in whatever sport. The courage you develop as an athlete will help you through the obstacles in life.

One of hockey's brightest stars, Mario Lemieux, recently faced a frightening battle with cancer. After treatment for Hodgkin's disease, Lemieux came back and got a goal and an assist during his first game. He attributed part of his recovery to his desire to return to hockey. "Anytime you have an injury like this, you have to have courage. But I didn't have any choice. It's my nature to fight back."

Being courageous, however, doesn't mean never being afraid. New adventures always involve some helpful degree of fear or anxiety. It can help you perform better.

When I played basketball, if I wasn't nervous before a game, it meant I was ill-prepared and would play poorly. Too much anxiety, on the other hand, immobilizes you. It upsets your rhythm and throws off your timing. Basketball players can usually sink free throws in practice when no one's watching. Yet sinking a free throw in the final second of a championship game before thousands, the score tied, it gets a little harder.

Instead of allowing anxiety to best you, consider it another opportunity to grow. Overcoming fear helps develop personal strength and the courage to go on.

### Experience

Experience is a great teacher. When you've done something once, you know you can do it again.

Sports gives you plenty of experience in overcoming obstacles—experience that can be called upon to help you overcome obstacles in other areas of your life.

In April 1980 Tracy Austin was the No. 1 tennis player in the world. Then sciatica (severe pain that occurs when a spinal disk presses on the sciatic nerve) felled her. The pain kept her bedridden for some time. Little by little, she worked her way back until she found herself playing in the 1981 U.S. Open finals against Martina Navratilova, losing badly.

Tracy was on the verge of giving up. But something happened. She decided she could either throw in the towel or fight back, point by point, little by little, as she had in her "match" against sciatic pain. She won.

Other obstacles plagued Austin's career, however. In 1989, after five years of hard work to recover from tennis injuries, she finally hit the courts again. Then, a serious car accident left her with a shattered knee. Physical therapy was agonizing.

"Sometimes I'd cry and beg the session to end," she recalled, "but I kept plugging away. I remembered my match against Martina eight years earlier when I'd won by fighting back point by point. I knew that what helped me win then—desire, discipline, and faith in myself—would get me back on my feet."

Tracy Austin called upon her experience to overcome athletic obstacles and regain the ability to walk. She knew she had overcome barriers in the past and that she'd do it again.

All athletes must learn how to handle setbacks and losses, to pick themselves up off the floor and get back into the contest. They learn, too, the necessity of doing whatever it takes to return either to their original goals and purpose or adapt to their new reality and move on to new purposes.

These lessons, put to good use, will give you a head start in dealing with the obstacles you will face in your post-sports world.

## Practice Time

*Never Give Up #1*

Inspire yourself by learning about athletes and others who have overcome obstacles in their lives. You can do this by reading one or more of the following books:

- *Helen Keller: From Tragedy to Triumph,*
  Aladdin Press, 1990
- Dave and Jan Dravecky, *When You Can't Come Back,*
  Zondervan Press, 1992
- Ryan White, *My Own Story,*
  Signet, 1992
- Jay Hoyle, *Mark: How a Boy's Courage in Facing AIDS Inspired a Town and the Town's Compassion Lit Up a Nation,*
  Langford Books, [Diamond Communications, Inc.] 1988

*Never Give Up #2*

Think of an obstacle that keeps you from becoming as successful as you would like. Some examples of such obstacles include: Fear of public speaking; fear of asking for a commitment (in a personal or business relationship); fear of going after something you really want. Using the techniques you learned on goal-setting, work to overcome this obstacle.

Whenever you feel like giving up, think about what it takes to push through hard times. Courage and perseverance can take you far. Remember how good it feels to push through and not give up. Go for it.

# 11

# MIXING IT UP
## The Racial and Cultural Diversity of Sports

### The Game Plan

In this chapter I will talk about:

• the positive and negative influence of sports on diversity
• two traits that threaten the success of human relations

*I would rather concentrate on the similarities of humans instead of their differences.*

*- Ann Landers*

Deep down, most of us know there's only one race—the human race.  In a perfect world, addressing the issue of racial and cultural diversity would be unnecessary.  This world, however, is far from perfect.

The sports world isn't perfect, either.  Not all that long ago, the PGA found itself in trouble for scheduling a golf tournament at a country club that denied membership to blacks.

Some people argue that sports—especially, the revenue-producers—exploit a certain group of athletes, namely, black athletes.  As evidence, they cite the large numbers of black athletes versus the small number of blacks in sports management.

Exploitation can take other forms, as well.  Grant Hill, a former star forward at Duke University and now a Detroit Piston, realized that his basketball prowess had set him apart from other blacks on campus.

"I know I get treated differently because I'm an athlete, and I don't experience a lot of things a lot of minority students here experience," he said.

"There is definitely a problem.  Duke talks about multiculturalism...[but] I don't see it, I really don't."

Despite these problems, I believe that, overall, the sports community does a better job than society at bringing people of diverse backgrounds together and promoting understanding of that diversity.

I've learned that preaching at people seldom changes human behavior and attitudes. Experience—learning for oneself—offers the greatest potential for change, and sports can provide this experience.

On a team, you and your teammates work toward a common goal. As you do, you come together. Even in individual sports, you share the same experiences with your competitors, and this builds a bridge between you. You know the training and effort they have put forth, the price they've paid to compete, the talent required. Respect and appreciation come easier.

Granted, the locker room is no different than the rest of society in that people tend to form groups and hang out with those who share similarities. But when you spend 25-30 hours a week together practicing and playing—when you share the same classes, the same goals, the same adjustments—it creates a bond.

Often this bond starts with children on the playground. Children learn very quickly to choose as teammates those athletes who are the best competitors, regardless of how they personally feel about them. I know this from experience. Growing up, I was often one of the few white kids at the park or in the gym. To top things off, I was Jewish, making me more of an oddity. On the basketball court, however, none of that mattered. All that mattered was that I performed.

## Stereotyping and Insensitivity: A Threat to Human Relations

Sports can provide a chance for people of diverse backgrounds to gain a better understanding of each other. We rarely take advantage of that opportunity, though. Stereotyping and insensitivity keeps us from developing an understanding of other races and cultures. These traits, alive in all people, constantly threaten the success of human relations.

What is stereotyping? When we make assumptions, or generalizations, about an individual or group of individuals, such as

"All Irish people have tempers," or, "All blacks are good athletes," or, "All women are moody when they have their periods," we promote a stereotype. We may think certain stereotypes are harmless or even funny, but, in the long run, stereotypes of any kind prevent us from knowing people as they really are.

Insensitivity is usually caused by well-meaning people who simply don't think. They don't realize that what they say or do (or don't say or do) in a particular circumstance might bother someone else. For an example of insensitivity at its greatest, one need look no further than Marge Schott, owner of the Cincinnati Reds. Schott was suspended for one year and fined $25,000 by Major League Baseball's executive council after it concluded she had made racial and ethnic slurs, including the use of the word "nigger."

The process of understanding and appreciating different races and cultures is twofold. First, you have to want to and, second, you have to battle stereotyping and insensitivity to achieve this want.

## Ahead of the Rest

The sports world is imperfect, but it is ahead of society in general when it comes to exposing us to diversity. It demonstrates that diversity can work. People can join together, put aside prejudices and differences to achieve a common goal. Athletics provide a wonderful laboratory for learning about diversity, assuming that there is communication and understanding.

Sports can do more than aid individuals to look beyond their differences and form satisfying interpersonal relationships. It can strengthen the very fabric of our social institutions and culture.

The challenge for the athlete is to improve the locker room experience of diversity and take it beyond the locker room.

## Practice Time

### *Building Bridges #1*
On one side of a piece of paper, make a list of as many racial and ethnic stereotypes as you can think of. On the other side, list why that particular stereotype could be hurtful. Do the same for the stereotypes stemming from weight, height, educational background.

### *Building Bridges #2*
Challenge your knowledge of other races or cultures by:

- reading books or articles, i.e. *There Are No Children Here*
- seeing a play or movie, i.e. *Schindler's List*
- mustering the courage to ask others questions about their culture, family, and race.

### *Building Bridges #3*
Practice putting yourself in another's shoes and seeing things through his or her eyes.

# 12
# PLAYING BY THE RULES
## Sportsmanship On and Off the Field

### The Game Plan

In this chapter I will talk about:

- sportsmanship
- the difference between sportsmanship and merely following the rules
- how sportsmanship on the field translates to sportsmanship in the real world

*There is no real excellence in all this world which can be separated from right living.*
- David Starr Jordan

*You've got do to what's honest and right. People forget the scores of basketball games; they don't ever forget what you're made of.*
- Rockdale County (GA) High's Cleveland Stroud who gave up his team's 1987 state title on a technicality

Sportsmanship was a common word when I was a kid. I remember seeing the well-known Grantland Rice quote ("It doesn't matter whether you win or lose, but how you play the game") on a plaque in the entrance to the Hollywood YMCA where my Long Beach "C" team traveled annually for a contest. That statement, together with another—"nobody likes a sore loser"—epitomized much of our playing philosophy.

Lately, sportsmanship hasn't been emphasized as it once was. (For numerous examples of this, see the upcoming sections on "Where Are Your Manners: Winning, Losing, and Playing With Class," and "Dancing in the End Zone: Why Playing to the Crowd Can Get You in Trouble.") A sad commentary. Sportsmanship is one of the greatest lessons that athletics has to teach.

As one young writer commented in an essay on sportsmanship: "It's how a person reacts to the wins and losses in life that is a huge part of defining who we are." Sports without sportsmanship is worse than having no sports at all.

## Defining Sportsmanship

*Sports nudged me, as it has a great part of our society, from the savage toward the humane. At least I hope it has, for to celebrate sports is to celebrate self-control.*
- Kenny Moore, former Olympic runner

Sportsmanship is hard to define. You always recognize it, though. It's helping a fallen opponent off the floor. Congratulating someone whether they beat you or you beat them. Most of all, I think sportsmanship is self-control.

Kenny Moore, a former Olympian, tells the following story about sportsmanship:

> In the state high school cross-country meet in my senior year, I started too fast and ambitiously sprinted myself into oxygen debt. I drifted, sick and disgusted, back into the pack. A crosstown rival, who had not beaten me all year, passed me at the finish. I used a wild elbow to try to keep him behind, but to no avail.
>
> That evening at dinner, my father remarked that my avowed concern for fairness and discipline seemed inconsistent with slugging opponents. I wanted to shout, "You win any way you can!" but I knew it was absurd. That was what football players said. I still remember the acid turmoil of that night, my mind frantically squirming to avoid the truth of what I had done. Ultimately, I could not. Out of this experience came a resolve that I would never again lose control, no matter what the goad.

One of my favorite stories regarding sportsmanship concerns

the father who saw his 14-year-old son sniping and arguing in a big tennis tournament. The father walked out onto the court, took the racket out of the boy's hand, and told him to go home. "Dad, I can *win* this match," the boy pleaded. To which his father responded, "I don't see how. You don't have a racket."

That young tennis player would have done better to follow Arthur Ashe's example. Ashe never let himself be goaded into unsportsmanlike behavior. He was a model of sportsmanship. In contrast to some of the tennis players who came after him— the Jimmy Connors and John McEnroes youngsters seem more inclined to emulate—he never resorted to boorish behavior. There was no cursing, no arguing with linesmen. He let his play say it all.

## Sportsmanship: More than Just Playing by the Rules

A lot of people would define sportsmanship as playing by the rules. To a point, that is true. It *is* important to play by the rules—sports teach that. Still, sometimes more is required. Sportsmanship is setting a standard for *living* and sticking to it. It means abiding by your life values. Sometimes that can be hard to do in the sports world. For example, a *Sports Illustrated* article on O.J. Simpson brought up the subject of the athlete's notorious womanizing. One of Simpson's colleagues from the broadcast field was quoted as saying, "...as you know, he's charming and he's in that athletic world that winks at that."

Not long ago, a newspaper featured an article on a Little League player who received a commendation for his honesty on the playing field. Apparently, an umpire had ruled the young boy "safe" in a controversial play. To everyone's amazement, the boy informed the umpire that he was not safe, that he'd felt the other player tag him out.

Among the many letters to the editor praising the boy for his integrity, was one from a man who said the boy had done the wrong thing. Playing by the rules, his letter insisted, meant going along with the umpire's call, right or wrong.

Technically, the man was right. But what about morally?

A sportswriter once commented that "sports are fundamentally unimportant except in the context of the values they teach." If values are the way things should be (in contrast to the way they often are), then the boy played by the higher "rule" of the true sportsman.

## Sportsmanship On and Off the Field

It stands to reason that the athlete who can exhibit sportsmanship, despite all the pressures of athletic competition, is more likely to exhibit sportsmanship in other aspects of life. People who are truly successful in life are the ones who live by a standard—who "play fair" in both their personal and professional lives.

I will again use Arthur Ashe as an example. Ashe always embodied good sportsmanship on the playing field. But if, as one writer said, "Sportsmanship is also an athlete's ability to shift from being a selfish competitor to being a useful member of society," then Arthur Ashe was the epitome of a sportsman. He was instrumental in getting South Africa banned from the Davis Cup competition because of its Apartheid policies. He led in the creation of minority youth tennis programs. He demonstrated on behalf of Haitian refugees. Finally, he became a spokesman for the millions of people suffering from AIDS.

In an article entitled "Is Sportsmanship Dead?" Peter Bodo, contributing editor of *Tennis* magazine, noted that in our Anglo-democratic society sports were originally intended to help create "the well-rounded gentleman." They were supposed to teach loyalty and leadership, balancing mental activities with physical exertion. But as sports became less of an amateur activity and more business-oriented, that focus was lost. Instead, you saw athletes who were more concerned with developing themselves as a product than as a person.

One of the hardest things to do these days is to be a good sport. Even the phrase, "Be a sport," has a negative connotation to it. But it isn't geeky or wimpy to be a sport—it's just the opposite. It shows that you have the strength of character to do what you know is right. It develops and reveals your true character.

Bobby Thomson, the New York Giants' baseball player who, in the final playoff game of the 1951 season, hit the game-winning home run that beat the Dodgers in "the shot heard 'round the world," never bragged about his feat. As a sportsman, it wasn't in his character.

Arthur Ashe never bragged about his tennis accomplishments. It wasn't in his character, either. Arthur Ashe died too soon. But he died as he lived—a sportsman—and we're all the richer for it.

## Practice Time

### *Be a Sport*

Hopefully, your athletic experience has taught you the importance of being a good sport. It is not something that comes easily, however; almost everyone can use some more work on their sportsmanship skills. Here are some ways you can get the practice you need:

- Challenge someone to a friendly game of whatever—tennis, chess, arm-wrestling—and *keep it friendly*. Whether you win or lose, congratulate the other person and compliment them on their ability. Then try to make this a habit in other areas of competition (i.e., school play try-outs, landing a new business account, etc.).
- Think about a cause important to you. Get involved in trying to make a difference in the world around you.
- Give compliments—in sports, in relationships, on the job.
- Be fair. You might lose the game or the match, but you will build a new level of character that will last all of your life.

# 13
# KEEPING YOUR EYE ON THE BALL
## The Hazards of Tunnel Vision

### The Game Plan

In this chapter I will talk about:

• what tunnel vision is
• how having tunnel vision can help you on the field
  (and hurt you off)
• why it's important to have balance in your life

In the book *Unfinished Business*, author Jack McCallum quotes this exchange between Boston Celtic coach Chris Ford and Kevin McHale:

> "What are you doing?" Ford asked McHale as the coach prepared to convene the pre-game meeting.
>
> "I'm brushing my teeth," McHale said. "What's it look like?"
>
> "We've got a game, you know," Ford said.
>
> "Well, ten years from now nobody will know who won this game," McHale said. "But I'll know if I have cavities."

What exactly is tunnel vision? Centering all your attention and efforts on one thing. In football, receivers need tunnel vision. All they're supposed to see is the ball. A couple of 210-pound defensive backs may be inches away from pounding them into the turf, but they don't see that. Their attention is fixed on that little scrap of inflated leather flying through the air. Catching it focuses all of their energies.

Tunnel vision is great for receivers meeting up with a pass. Off the playing field, however, tunnel vision might work to limit your knowledge and experience of the world around you.

A friend related a story that illustrates the latter kind of tunnel vision. He watched the 1992 Democratic National Convention, engrossed in the powerful speeches being given. In the middle of the proceedings, he received a call from another part of the country—a coaching friend of his at a youth sports camp. After talking about the various activities taking place at the camp, the coach asked the friend what he was doing.

"Watching the convention," was my friend's reply.

"Oh." Silence. "What convention?"

## Focus vs. Balance

To excel at something usually means spending a lot of time at it. Sometimes it requires sacrifices—giving up a social life, cutting back on other activities, or spending less time with your family. Athletes call this concentration "being focused." Another word for it is "tunnel vision."

A drawback to tunnel vision is that it often indicates a life out of balance. This happens to many athletes. They think having a balanced life means putting less intensity into their sport; that it means loss of focus. However, it is possible to have great focus without having tunnel vision. It requires the ability to concentrate on one thing and then step back and see how that applies to the big picture.

Take someone such as Nolan Ryan, for example. The man played baseball until he was old as Methusulah, so you know he had to be pretty good at maintaining his focus. At the same time, he wasn't just a ballplayer; he was a bank owner. That meant being aware of monetary policies, financial trends, and so on. It meant being able to step back from baseball to see what was happening in the real world.

Other players don't bother to do that. During former 49ers quarterback Joe Montana's long recovery and rehabilitation from back surgery, he was asked once about retirement. He couldn't think about it, he answered, because it would distract him from focusing on getting ready to play.

To me, Joe's answer was just another way of saying, "I can't think about the future because I'm too busy worrying about the present." In the long run, that can be a destructive attitude—but one Montana has avoided. On April 18, 1995, he formally announced his retirement, saying "I've got a lot of new things happening in my life I'm excited about."

Todd Williams is another athlete who gave up balance for focus. He wants to become one of the world's best distance runners. As someone who once trained with Williams said, "He can be a little hard to be around because everything has to be about running. Todd cuts out a lot of things that normal people do because he won't let anything get in the way of his running."

## The Need for Balance

At some point, however, the curve changes. Other things become important, as well. Tom "Satch" Sanders, former Boston Celtic and now Vice President of Player Programs for the NBA, once told me that the beginning of his desire for a more balanced life came "after my first sip of a high quality wine on a date with a very special woman." In other words, he saw more to care about in life than sports. As one college football star said, explaining his devotion to his studies, "Football may get me to the next level for a while, but it won't prepare me for the future. Without education, I may get the American Dream and not know how to handle it."

You can be a successful athlete without completely sacrificing other areas of your life. I've known athletes who have done it. The young baseball player who no one thought would get drafted because he had made it clear he was planning to serve a mission for his church (he did get drafted, and he still plans to serve.) The high school athlete—a letterman in three sports—who managed to star in the school play and court his future wife. The college football star who made the Dean's List as an electrical engineering major. Athletes, such as Steve Young, who couldn't be bothered with the controversy over who would be the 49ers' top quarterback, because he was busy taking his law finals at BYU.

Working to achieve a balanced life is difficult, for athletes or anyone. Finding balance isn't easy. Yet, finding balance in your life—avoiding the trap of tunnel vision—will help you gain the most out of your sports experience and save you from becoming a casualty of sports.

## Practice Time

Just as you have to practice making the positive lessons of sports a part of your everyday life, you need to also practice avoiding the negative lessons of sports. Here are some exercises to help you overcome the tunnel vision habit and achieve a more balanced life:

### Balancing Act #1

The opposite of tunnel vision is the ability to "see the whole field." Review the activities listed in the section on "Getting the Big Picture." If you have not yet incorporated these activities into your life, start now!

### Balancing Act #2

Keep a daily activity log for one week. Record what you do and how much time you spend doing it. Your log might look something like this:

Monday

| | |
|---|---|
| get ready for school: | 1/2 hour |
| classes: | 4 hours |
| studying: | 1/2 hour |
| practice: | 2 hours |
| talk with friends: | 1 hour |
| talk with parents: | 20 minutes |
| watch TV: | 1 hour |

At the end of the week, review your log. What do you spend most of your time doing? What do you spend the least time doing? Are there areas you would like to change? How might you do this? What effect would it have on your life?

You might try making a list of the things you need to do, as well as the things you want to do. (You can include life goals, as well as daily goals.) Now put an "A" by those things that are your top priority, a "B" by the things that are of secondary importance, and a "C" by the least important items. Compare these lists to your daily activity log. Are you spending the majority of your time doing the "A" and "B" items? If you see things you need to change, then develop an action plan, set some dates, and get to work!

# 14
# I AM THE GREATEST
## Puncturing the Inflated Ego

## The Game Plan

In this chapter I will talk about:

- the importance of having a healthy self-esteem
- how sports help build your ego
- the dangers of basing your self-esteem on your
  athletic prowess

*Making the transition from sports to the real world isn't as hard if the athlete doesn't retain delusions of grandeur. He must learn to show up on time for appointments. He must be responsible for the promises he makes. And he must learn to live without a team press agent, sheltering him and opening doors for him. It's an adjustment many athletes aren't prepared for.*
- Vince Evans, former quarterback with the Los Angeles Raiders

*Leaving football was hard for O.J. "What would I do with my time? What was I going to do to feed my ego now?"*
- "Simpson and Sudden Death," *U.S. News & World Report,* June 27, 1994

    Athletes are known for their extremely healthy egos. Ty Cobb was no exception. A reporter once interviewed Cobb many years after he had retired from the major leagues, where he established a lifetime batting average of .367. The reporter asked Cobb how he thought he would do against modern-day pitchers. Cobb allowed that he would bat only around .300. When the reporter expressed surprise, Cobb replied, "I don't think that's so bad, after all, I'm over 70 years old."

    Then there's the story of the Notre Dame football player back in the 1940s who was subpoenaed to appear in court as part of a civil suit. As he was sworn in, the judge asked, "Haven't I heard your name before?" The young man mentioned that he played football for Notre Dame, upon which the judge asked, "How good are you?"

The young man replied, "The best tackle Notre Dame has ever had."

When the boy's coach heard about the incident, he was furious over the youth's lack of modesty. Calling the young man into his office, he thundered, "How could you say such a thing?"

The kid's reply? "Gee Coach, I hated to do it — but after all, I *was* under oath."

Athletes have to have a lot of confidence. There's nothing wrong with that. It's called self-esteem.

Self-esteem is the relationship you have with yourself. This relationship cannot be underestimated. Dr. Joyce Brothers said, "Self-esteem determines the mate we attract, the career we have, the income we earn, the lifestyle we have, the type and quality of friends we have, the treatment we receive from people, the kind of health we enjoy." The healthier our self-esteem is, the better our life is likely to be.

Self-esteem is how you feel about yourself—how you "esteem" yourself. Self-esteem doesn't depend simply on what kind of person you think you are; it's also affected by what others say, think, and feel about you. If you grow up in a home with abusive parents who constantly give you the impression you are worthless, you may come to believe that you *are* worthless. If you grow up in a home with parents who love you and tell you that you can accomplish anything in life, then that is what you will probably believe about yourself.

## When Self-Esteem Gets Out of Control

The good thing about sports is that they can help boost your self-esteem. Performing well at a thing helps you to feel good about yourself. The bad thing about sports is that sometimes they can boost a person's self-esteem too much, and for all the wrong reasons.

It's easy to start thinking that maybe you are better than other people with hundreds, thousands, or even millions of people shouting your praises. What too few athletes realize is that the public's view of them has little to do with who they really are. The feedback athletes receive is in response to the role they play; not them, the individual. This is why it's easy for athletes to fall into the trap of "believing their press clippings," so to speak. As Dave Cowens, former player and coach for the Boston Celtics and now an assistant coach with the San Antonio Spurs, said, "You think about being idolized because you're a basketball player. It's absurd. A basketball player is nothing important. He doesn't really contribute to making people's lives happier—not like a plumber, fireman, or even a businessman."

## Pride Goes Before a Fall

There is another reason why it's dangerous to let athletic success go to your head: You won't always be an athlete. A singer can be a singer just about forever (at least, Frank Sinatra thinks so). A doctor can go on doctoring until the old stethoscope gives out. But a person is an athlete for only a very short time and then it's back to the real world. As I've stated before, the transition can be a shock. If your ego revolves around being an athlete, what happens when that is taken away from you?

One former football player commented, "It's a shame professional athletes don't have to deal with real life first. I mean like having a Joe Lunchbucket job and trying to make ends meet. That way they could really appreciate what a gift it is to play in the NFL, what a fairy-tale world it is."

## A Self-Esteem Quiz

How do you know if you are too dependent on your athletic skills? Ask yourself the following questions:

• Do I define myself in terms of athletic success?
• Do I equate being a great athlete with being a great person?
• Do I base my identity and self-worth on my athletic talent?
• What kind of person would I be if I didn't have athletic ability?

After a potentially career-ending knee injury, defensive tackle Keith Millard told *Sports Illustrated*, "Football has given me everything: Identity, money, confidence, friendships. I wonder what kind of man I would be without it."

The problem with basing your self-esteem on your athletic ability is that talents like this tend to be God-given, not necessarily anything you've created. If you base your identity on your talent, you're likely to have difficulty in non-athletic situations where your self-esteem may be diminished or even absent.

Athletes successful at an early age usually have few peers and are seldom threatened. It's unfortunate that all the attention and success an athlete receives can have the effect of inflating even the most modest egos because we all know what happens to inflation—eventually, deflation occurs. As the high school star becomes the college freshman, or the college standout becomes the professional rookie, the experience of competing against others who are equally endowed can be more traumatic than for those with less natural talents who long ago learned to operate efficiently under the stress of competition.

Letting athletic success go to your head, then, can get you into trouble in more ways than one. It may give you a sports-derived self-esteem that disappears when your athletic career ends. It can make it harder for you to compete when you come up against others with equal or better skills than your own. And, finally, it might drive people away from you.

In the Bible, the sin of idolatry is much more than a simple matter of bowing down to statues. Idol worship confuses the work of your own hands with the works of the divine. The Second Commandment reads, "You shall not make yourself a graven image." One commentator takes that to mean, "You shall not make an idol of yourself," rather than the traditional "for yourself." In other words, don't turn yourself into an object of worship—or you may find yourself worshipping alone.

## Practice Time

Your ego is more likely to get out of control when too much of your identity is tied up with being an athlete. To determine if this is a problem in your life, complete the following Athletic Identity Exercise:

Imagine a large circle. This circle represents you. Within the large circle is another, smaller circle. The small circle represents the core of your self—those characteristics that are always part of you, no matter what role you are playing. You will be asked to fill in the large circle with additional circles that represent what can be thought of as "sub-selves." The size of the circles you draw should reflect their importance in your life at this point in time.

### YOUR LIFE AS IT IS NOW

1. Begin by drawing a circle that represents your athletic "self."

2. Next, draw circles to represent each of the following aspects of yourself (leave out any that may not apply to you at this moment in your life or add others not shown on the list):

| | | |
|---|---|---|
| daughter/son | friend | worker |
| sibling | man/woman | lover |
| parent | student | hobbyist |
| citizen | believer | |

3. In each of the circles you have drawn, write the average number of hours per week you spend in activities that enhance that aspect of yourself.

### YOUR LIFE AS YOU WOULD LIKE IT TO BE

4. Now repeat steps 1-3, however, instead of drawing the diagram to reflect your life as is, draw it to reflect your life as you'd like it to be. Some circles will be larger; others, smaller. As you enter numbers in the circles, write the numbers of hours per week you would *like* to spend developing those areas of yourself.

5.   Do you experience any frustration or pain because you've been unable to more fully develop certain aspects of yourself? Elaborate.

6.   What would you need to do to move toward your ideal? Which aspects of yourself would you most like to change?

## YOUR LIFE AS OTHERS WOULD LIKE IT TO BE

7.   If the significant others in your life (coach, parents, spouse, etc.) could change you, how would they draw your self diagram? If the "ideal you" of others differs from your "ideal you," how do you deal with these differences in expectations?

## UNDERSTANDING YOUR CORE

8.   What characteristics make up your "core self"? List the three most dominant characteristics (i.e., stubbornness, generosity, humor, sensitivity, serious, hard working)

9.   How do these core characteristics reveal themselves in your athletic "self" using this analysis?

10. How are your athletic experiences affecting or influencing your core "self"?

11. As a result of this exercise, what steps do you feel you need to make to achieve your life objectives?

12. When you make the transition from the athletic world to the real world, how do you anticipate your definition of yourself will be impacted?

13. What can you do at this point in time to make this transition easier?

# 15
# IN SEARCH OF THE PERFECT "10"
## The Drawbacks of Perfectionism

### The Game Plan

In this chapter I will talk about:

• how sports promote perfectionism
• why striving for perfection isn't always the "perfect" thing to do
• how to tell if you're a perfectionist

*Good enough never is.*
### - Mrs. Fields

Debbie Fields has parlayed her motto, "Good enough never is," into a multi-million dollar cookie business.

"Good enough never is" could also be the rallying cry for perfectionists around the world. Because that's what a perfectionist often believes: No matter how well they've done something, they always could have done it a bit better.

On the face of it, you wouldn't think that perfectionism is such a bad thing. What's wrong with trying to be the best there is? What's the problem with trying to play the perfect game, achieve the perfect grade-point average, build the perfect body? After all, isn't that what we're suppose to be doing—striving for excellence? Isn't that what makes a person successful?

Yes...and no.

I've known a lot of athletes who have had a problem with perfectionism. The competitiveness of sports, as well as its very public-ness (no one likes to look bad in public) contribute to an athlete's need to be perfect.

So, athletes work and sweat and fight and train until they are very, very good at what they do. Yet sometimes they still don't feel like they measure up, so they endanger their lives in the quest for perfection. A football player takes steroids. A gymnast stays trim by vomiting after meals.

Another problem that comes with being exceptionally good in one area (athletics) is that it might prove hard to accept that you might not be as good in other areas. This problem is often reinforced by fans who love you when you're performing well and hate you when you're not. You begin to think people only love you when you're perfect.

## Too Perfect for Your Own Good

*Perfect is the enemy of the good.*
- Unknown

In striving for excellence, it is possible to be too perfect for your own good. In their book, *Real World 101*, James Caland and Jeff Salzman write that people can take one of two approaches towards achieving excellence: Neurotic perfection or practical perfection.

Neurotic perfectionists never finish and their work never is quite right. As a result, they live with high anxiety and low productivity. Their mistakes devastate them. Neurotic perfectionism can lead to health disorders, destroy relationships, and, otherwise, stop you from enjoying life. Someone who is a neurotic perfectionist is constantly searching for the ideal or perfect self. That person doesn't exist and never will.

Practical perfectionists, like neurotic ones, are also detail-oriented and committed to excellence. They realize, though, when something is "good enough" to achieve its purpose—even if it falls short of perfection. Practical perfectionists know that the standards they set for themselves won't always work for others. They appreciate other people, flaws and all. They refuse to beat up on themselves or someone else for not being perfect.

John Wooden knows something about perfection. His UCLA Bruin teams dominated the NCAA basketball scene for 15 years. Yet Wooden never harped on maintaining perfect records. Even during an undefeated season, the focus wasn't on staying undefeated. John knew that would only make his players more anxious than they already were.

If you must be a perfectionist, try being practical about it.

Do your best work, but know when to say enough is enough. Realize that improvement comes not only from learning *how* to do something, but also from learning how *not* to do something. Mistakes can be one of life's greatest learning tools.

## Are You a Perfectionist?

How can you tell if you are an out-and-out perfectionist, or merely someone who sets and strives for a high standard in life? Here are three questions to ask yourself:

1) *Am I trying to do my best or to be the best?*
Neurotic perfectionists struggle to reach impossible goals. Those who pursue excellence seek high but attainable goals. They also recognize the need for keeping those goals flexible.

2) *What drives me? Is it the desire for success or the fear of failure?*
Neurotic perfectionists remember mistakes and dwell on them. Sometimes they become so afraid of making the mistake again that they just stop trying. Seekers of excellence correct mistakes and learn from them.

3) *Am I enjoying the journey or focusing on the outcome?*
Neurotic perfectionists focus on what they do while seekers of excellence fix on who they *are*. A neurotic perfectionist is obsessed with external rewards and measurements—a trophy, a blue ribbon, straight A's on a report card. A seeker of excellence says, "OK, I didn't win first place, but I did improve my time and I gave my best effort."

## Practice Time

If you feel you are a neurotic perfectionist rather than a practical perfectionist, then you need to practice loosening up a bit. Try one of the following exercises:

### *Loosening Up #1*
Neurotic perfectionists have trouble completing projects because they never feel their work is quite good enough. If you have a project looming on the horizon (a term paper, a business report, a remodeling project), set a deadline for completion and stick to it. Do your best and don't sweat the small stuff. The more you do this, the easier it will get.

### *Loosening Up #2*
Because you have excelled in the athletic arena, you may be afraid to attempt something new (fearing that you will not be as good as you were in sports). One way to practice embracing the unfamiliar (and possibly making a fool of yourself) is to play games—charades, Pictionary, Read My Lips, are a few that come to mind.

# 16

# WHERE ARE YOUR MANNERS?
## Winning, Losing, and Playing with Class

### The Game Plan

In this chapter I will talk about:

- today's trend toward poor sportsmanship
- some examples of sportsmanship at its lowest
- how good manners can help you be a better competitor

*I really regret that there is an attitude that apparently permeates society today that if you have certain athletic skills, then that stands as an excuse for your conduct. We've got to draw the line somewhere. This excusability concept has got to stop.*
        *- U.S. District Judge Elizabeth Kovachevich*

*The younger players have brought that playground mentality. We didn't used to go out there and taunt. When I came in, you didn't have time to taunt.*

*You think with Moses Malone and Rudy Tomjanovich and Maurice Lucas, I could have gotten away with activity like a little kid? We had to be grown men like them.*
        *- Former Houston Rockets forward Robert Reid*

At one tennis tournament in Florida, hampered by rain and severe weather changes that made the stadium court unplayable for two days, some players let their tempers get the best of them. They griped about the facilities, the weather (as if anyone could do anything about it), the fans, the tournament umpires and staff, and one top-seeded player even walked out on the tournament.

What these players lost sight of was that many people in Florida still lived in tents (thanks to Hurricane Andrew), while they sat around in relative, although boring, comfort. And got paid for it!

Unfortunately, the sight of ill-mannered athletes is all too common these days. The word "sportsmanship" is, increasingly, preceded by the adjective "poor." Why is this?

Two reasons come to my mind. One, athletic training rarely teaches athletes how to play fair. When they're on the field, athletes often see rules as obstacles to get around. Off the field, the second reason for athletes' lack of manners comes into play: the special treatment athletes receive. This treatment sometimes give athletes the impression that the rules governing society don't apply to them. This can lead to breaking the rules in a big way.

In recent years, star athletes have found themselves in trouble for everything from illegal gambling, tax fraud, and drug possession to assault, carrying a concealed weapon, and murder. Sports are no guarantee of virtue, but neither are they meant to shield successful athletes from social and ethical responsibilities.

## No Hand Outs

*If we're afraid to let athletes shake hands, we're in really bad shape.*
- Larry Aubry, a 27-year member of the Los Angeles Human
  Relations Committee

A disturbing trend in the sports world today is the banning of the post-game handshake. Why are sports officials giving the thumbs-down to this longtime symbol of sportsmanship? Because they are afraid of the reactions this supposedly innocent gesture sometimes provokes. Athletes have been known to spit on their hands before shaking, or to add a few choice words to make sure their true sentiments are known. Sometimes handshakes have even led to fistfights.

Proponents of the ban argue that, in addition to the safety issue, the post-game handshake is not really sportsmanship—it's just something that athletes do because they're expected to do it. There's no real feeling behind it. I imagine that's often true. But does that mean we should only hold a door open for another person when we feel like it? Or give up our seat on the bus just to those persons we're fond of?

I'm sure Miss Manners would agree that good manners often have nothing to do with good feelings. The essence of good manners is doing the right thing whether we feel like it or not. The essence of sportsmanship is the same.

## Trash Talking

When you can walk the walk, you don't need to talk the talk.

A frequently witnessed display of bad manners these days is what is referred to as "trash talking." Other words for it include "woofing," "barking," or "huffing." It's the playground equivalent of informing an opponent that his mother wears army boots. The intent is to throw off an opponent's timing, causing him or her to mess up a play or play poorly. As sportswriter, Ira Berkow, related in *The New York Times*; however, the tactic sometimes backfires:

> A few years ago, in a tight game in the final minute of the NCAA West Regional, Paris McCurdy of Ball State, stepped to the free-throw line. Greg Anthony of Nevada-Las Vegas, hoping to throw him off his game, sauntered behind him and said quietly, "You're going to shoot another one of those bricks, man." McCurdy said, "We'll see." Anthony said, "Your mama can shoot better free throws than you." McCurdy said, "Ain't got no mama."
>
> A strange look came over Anthony's face, and he walked away silently. A little smile appeared on McCurdy's face—for, in fact, he did have a mother. He also sank both free throws...

Trash talk on the playing field is a controversial subject. Some view it with tolerance or even amusement. One sportswriter came to the defense of the University of Michigan's trash-talking team by saying, "College coaches are allowed—required

—to taunt, curse, bark, woof, emote, and do silly dances. But if players resort to any of this foolishness, they're out of control." Others, like John Wooden, think players and coaches should practice a certain decorum on the field.

The controversy reminds me of my own painful experience as a young athlete. On one hand, you have a strong person who takes the taunts thrown at him and uses them as fuel for a stronger performance—the "I'll show them" attitude. It lifts their game.

At the other end of the scale are those individuals whose development has not reached such heights of confidence. They are the ones who are adversely affected by this kind of poor sportsmanship and the effects go beyond just the game.

One other problem with trash talk is that it can turn into something more. As Ira Berkow said, "The possible escalation of pushing an opponent verbally is to punch him." When talk show host Jim Rome repeatedly called Jim Everett "Chris Evert" during a televised interview, Everett responded by pushing over a table and attacking Rome. (The only person who showed any semblance of good manners over the incident was the real-life Chris Evert, who responded: "The whole episode was very unprofessional, but at eight-months pregnant I have more important things to discuss."

The unfortunate fact is that we live in an increasingly violent world. Whether sports contribute to that violence or only mirror it is a subject of debate. What I do know is that athletes can be powerful role models in the fight against violence. This means resisting the pressure to use trash talk "because everyone else is doing it." It means seeing your opponent as an opponent, not as an enemy. It means concentrating on winning, not on getting in the most verbal cracks.

Former NBA superstar Bill Walton decried the violence that he sees in sports today. "Players have gotten away from understanding that winning is the ultimate barometer," he said. "There's too much emphasis on individual match-ups, the stat sheet, making the spectacular play. And did I say the money? If players thought about how important the winning is, and concentrate on the drive to win, a lot of this stuff would go away."

The bottom line is, trash talk has no place in sports. It's not the high road. Nor is it the best of what sports can and should be.

## The Saga of Schottsie

Of course, the argument might be made, "How can you expect players to be well mannered when the people around them—coaches, owners, etc.—are setting such a poor example?" Which brings us to Marge Schott, owner of the Cincinnati Reds.

Schott became the target of an investigation after Tim Sabor, a former Reds financial officer, made charges in a suit against her. He stated in a deposition that Schott routinely used racial slurs and ordered him not to hire minority personnel. Sharon Jones, a former official with the Oakland Athletics, also accused Schott of making racist comments about African-Americans and, while on a telephone conference call with fellow owners in 1987, vowing never to hire one.

Schott went on to deny most of the charges made against her, but acknowledged other complaints, such as keeping a swastika as a souvenir. Eventually, Mrs. Schott was fined and put on probation.

The Marge Schott issue divided people into two main camps: Those who thought what she said was disgusting and should be punished; and those who thought what she said was disgusting, but that she had every right to freely express her views.

The subject we are talking about, however, is not freedom of speech—it is good manners. I think there can be no question that Marge Schott displayed an appalling lack of manners. As writer Doug Krikorian, stated in the *Long Beach Press-Telegram*, "Baseball advertises itself as the national pastime, and it's a high-profile sport in which human beings of all colors are heavily involved in its operation…Baseball ownership is an intrinsic part of the public domain…and there is a certain decorum she is expected to maintain in these racially divisive times in light of such a unique position of influence."

## Minding Your P's and Q's

Are manners really that important? Yes, they are. As the world becomes more and more technological, the importance of the "human touch" cannot be underestimated. In addition, as businesses become more global, the need for people who can communicate sensitively with other cultures multiplies. According to etiquette expert, Letitia Baldridge, the successful people in the 1990s will take the time to use good manners because it will impress people in our increasingly crowded and impersonal world.

Manners are more than just good behavior. Ms. Baldridge states that: "Manners are based on the bedrock of good character, which translates into kindness, compassion, thoughtfulness… and, yes, respect for others…They show that you care about the other person's dignity and feelings, no matter who that person is."

## Good Manners: Your Competitive Edge

A lot of athletes might believe that they can't be competitive and mannerly at the same time. They couldn't be more wrong. Competition, in the true sense of the word, doesn't grind an opponent into the dust. It means playing with, not against, your opponent, using each other's accomplishments to inspire. It requires the both of you to do and act your best.

The word "competitor" should be a positive term. A person who is a competitor can lose but still be a winner, because:

• they did their best
• they had a good experience
• they learned or grew from the experience
• they handled defeat well

Competition in sports is often a metaphor for, a reflection of, and preparation for, competition in real life. Our society is based on competition. It's called the free market system. It's difficult to succeed in our world without a competitive spirit, and this is an edge that sports give you.

But good manners also give you an edge in this competitive world. They endow you with self-confidence. They give others confidence in you. Ultimately, they make you a better person and the world a better place. Imagine what it would be like if everyone toned down their rhetoric, cleaned up their talk, and put a monitor on their attitude!

## Practice Time

### *To the Manner Born #1*

Good manners don't come naturally; they're learned. Two good books to read on the subject are: *Complete Guide to Executive Manners* and *The Manners for the 90s* by Letitia Baldridge.

### *To the Manner Born #2*

Practice good manners. For example, if making introductions is difficult for you, practice in front of a mirror. Listen to how you sound, what you do. Work on improving your technique. Don't be afraid to let people see you as a warm and caring person. After all, good personality reflects a good person.

### *To the Manner Born #3*

Before attending an evening you expect to make you nervous, rehearse. Visualize yourself making introductions, shaking hands, opening conversations. (This kind of visualization should be very familiar to you as an athlete!)

# 17
# DANCING IN THE END ZONE
## (or: Why Playing to the Crowd Can Get You in Trouble)

## The Game Plan

In this chapter I will talk about:

• why more athletes are "dancing in the end zone"
• three reasons why dancing in the end zone can backfire on you
• how immaturity in athletes promotes "end zone dancing"

*I like the beauty of the game, the finesse, the maneuverability. Not showmanship.*
   - John Wooden

Once upon a time, people went to sporting events to watch the athletes play. Now they go to watch them perform. With millions—even billions—of dollars at stake, and round-the-clock television coverage of just about any sport you could ask for, athletes have to be more than just good to catch the eye of the public. They have to be entertainers. As Albert Lewis, cornerback for the Kansas City Chiefs, put it, "The days of scoring a touchdown and throwing the ball to the official are over. When a guy scores now, he is promoting something for TV, a new dance. It's for marketing."

Not everyone agrees with the philosophy behind the "new improved" athlete. John Wooden, talking about some of the pyrotechnics that go on these days in basketball games, said, "I don't like the dunk. I think it's hurt the game rather than helped. But fans love it. I have noticed that when there is a fancy dunk in a game, the fans just roar. You run a nice play and get an easy basket, and there's just a smattering of applause."

**107**

## Why Dancing in the End Zone Can Backfire

Dancing in the end zone may play well for the cameras, but sometimes you can end up tripping over your feet. Here are three circumstances when dancing in the end zone can sometimes backfire:

### 1) *Counting Your Chickens Before They're Hatched*

Remember Super Bowl XXVII? A Dallas Cowboy lineman ran for the end zone, the ball in his hands, a touchdown a sure thing. So he thought. As he ran with outstretched hands, he acknowledged the cheers of the crowd. Then an opponent surprised him from behind and knocked the ball from his hands. While the lost touchdown was meaningless in a game the Cowboys had already won, it was, in all probability, this man's only chance to ever score a Super Bowl touchdown. And he blew it.

The moral of the story: Don't take anything for granted—a touchdown, a relationship, a customer, a boss. Don't goof off while the serious chat with your spouse is going on. Ring up the sale *after* the money's in hand. Don't count your chickens before they're hatched.

### 2) *Fan Backlash*

A letter to the editor of *Sports Illustrated* read: "How I yearn for a touchdown without the dance, for a sack or tackle without the arms up. Please leave your helmet on. Go back to the huddle. Play the game. Let me decide if I wish to cheer you for doing that for which you are overpaid. I love the games but am getting sick of the athletes."

It is true that many fans enjoy—even applaud—the athlete who puts on a "good show." But it is also true that many others are becoming increasingly disillusioned with the antics of athletes on and off the field.

In the real world, backlash against the person who is constantly showing off can have serious consequences. It can result in loss of friendship, a lack of business opportunities—even destroy marriages and family relationships.

### 3) *The Poor Sport*

One reporter noted that Deion Sanders, now of the San

Francisco 49ers, high-steps the final 20 yards of a touchdown just to embarrass the players chasing him.

Remember what we talked about in the last section? Sportsmanship is more than being a good loser—it's being a good winner, too. Okay—so maybe it's too much to expect athletes in the heat of competition to help a fallen opponent off the ground. But is it too much to expect them to refrain from dancing over the opponent?

Poor sportsmanship never pays off. On the playing field, it can serve to spur an opponent on to even greater effort. Off the playing field, it does the same. In addition, where poor sports in athletics are often tolerated, in the real world they're not.

## The Struggle for Maturity

*The human race, to which so many of my readers belong, has been playing at children's games from the beginning, which is a nuisance for the few who grow up.*
- G.K. Chesterton, 1904

We know some of the rationale behind dancing in the end zone. Athletes promoting themselves, clowning for the fans' approval. But one of the main reasons behind the "dancing in the end zone" syndrome is that athletes who do it are immature.

One cannot address the subject of showboating, the end zone strut, or whatever you call it, without reflecting on the underlying theme of immaturity in athletes.

When athletic identity is too large a part of your total identity (as we've discussed is often the case with athletes), it fosters immaturity and naiveté. Focusing so much attention on the athletic self allows the other areas of your life to go underdeveloped. You may fail to see the consequences of your actions. You may lack sophistication, perception, and common sense.

You can achieve success, lots of money, and still be naive. Martina Navratilova claimed that her naiveté led her to sign a cohabitation agreement with her former lover—an agreement that brought her emotional and financial harm. Pete Rose's naiveté allowed him to believe he could associate with the shadiest of characters and come out smelling like...well, a rose. O.J. Simpson had dreams of being as big a star on the movie screen as he was on the football field. One writer said these fantasies revealed how "naive and sheltered" O.J. really was.

To mature, you need introspection and self-evaluation. You must want to grow up emotionally. You can't emulate relief pitcher Rob Dibble of the Cincinnati Reds, who tends to throw baseballs at hitters when he gets upset. For a guy with a 95 MPH fastball, that's a dangerous way to let off steam.

What is maturity? It's not something we wake up one morning and suddenly discover in ourselves. Rather, it's a continuing life process marked by the ability to get along with others; to display a reasonable amount of self-sufficiency; to set realistic goals; to exercise discretion; to differentiate between the important and the unimportant; and to show adaptability, flexibility, and stability.

## The Four Types of Maturity

There are four types of maturity: Intellectual, social, moral, and emotional. Intellectual maturity involves the ability to form your own opinions, to respect the opinions of others, to make your own decisions, and to change your mind in light of new evidence. Social maturity allows us to reach out to others, to have meaningful relationships, to be capable of independence and interdependence. Moral maturity grounds us in believing in and living by clearly defined moral standards.

The fourth type, emotional maturity, is the one I think is most important. The emotionally mature person is more likely to exhibit maturity in other areas. Dr. Aaron Stern, in his book *Me: The Narcissistic American,* defines emotional maturity as "the ability to live with uncertainty and the ability to delay gratification in favor of long-range goals." Unfortunately, the athletic lifestyle hinders the development of these abilities. This is one reason why so many athletes exhibit the emotional maturity of children, rather than adults.

The amount of time spent in sports, the intensity of focus, single-mindedness, and the protection from resulting consequences are all serious barriers preventing the athlete from pro-gressing through the normal life stages of growth and develop-ment. Instead of moving through childhood, adolescence, early adulthood and on, confronting the issues and tasks of each stage, the athlete often gets hung up in adolescence.

Most of life's choices are still open to you throughout adult-hood. The game of life is far from complete. The problem is that having been emotionally arrested in adolescence, the athlete enters the second half of the season some 15-20 games off the pace without the skills and abilities to catch up. In short, the ath-lete continues to be influenced by the patterns, decisions, and experiences of his or her youth. Does this mean you are destined to settle for a life of immaturity and incompleteness? Of course not. Part of the struggle to succeed in the adult world involves recognizing early patterns and decisions that were inappropriate or harmful, and realizing that you can change them. It means questioning the messages and meanings attached to these earlier experiences and acquiring new beliefs, thoughts, or values that work in the new ballgame—the real world.

At the end of your athletic career, many choices will have to be made. For example, choosing a new career field or a school to attend. Other choices might involve what kind of role you're going to play in your family now that sports no longer demand your time and attention. The temptation to let others make these choices for you might be great. But if you truly desire successful, mature adulthood, you'll ignore that temptation and take the responsibility for your own choices. You'll choose to stop dancing in the end zone and start exercising control over your actions.

## Practice Time

### *Measuring Up*

How mature are you? The following questions provide some yardsticks for measuring emotional maturity:

1.  How do you deal with reality? Do you face it or run from it? The emotionally mature individual faces up to the realities of life.

2.  How easily are you able to change?

3.  How do you manage your anxiety?

4.  Do you give more than you take?

5.  Do you have the necessary people skills to succeed off the playing field?

6.  Are you able to control destructive impulses—those sudden urges to explode in anger, drive too fast, drink too much, etc.?

7.  How much can you love? The more mature you are, the more capacity you have to love other people.

   After answering the questions, do you see areas where you need to improve?

# 18
# HANGING UP THE GLOVES
## Dealing with Aggressive Behavior

### The Game Plan

In this chapter I will talk about:

- why aggressiveness is an important quality for athletes to have
- what happens when aggressiveness is carried too far
- the difference between being aggressive and being assertive

*I've got a short fuse, a real short fuse. I've got to work to keep it quiet. When it goes off, I enjoy it when I'm in it, then I feel badly that it happened. I might grab somebody, do anything. I'm a nice guy. I really am. But I've got to work at it. I'm a mean guy inside.*
- a baseball manager speaking to the press

*I had a license to kill sixty minutes a week. It was like going totally insane. The best lineman were all sadistic.*
- Alex Karras, former Detroit Lions defensive tackle

Being aggressive when the situation calls for it is part of being an athlete. When Shawn Bradley returned from a two-year Mormon mission in Australia, some scouts expressed concern that someone who spent years preaching love and kindness still had the necessary "meanness" to make it in the NBA—even if that someone did stand 7 feet 6 inches tall.

Without that aggressive spirit, that "fire in the belly," it's difficult, if not impossible, to be a successful athlete. Just ask Walt Patulski. As a defensive end from Notre Dame, Patulski was the No. 1 draft pick in 1972. His career, though, never lived up to its initial promise. Part of the reason: his lack of aggression. "I was a great guy...I am a great guy," Patulski said. "I was always the guy who you would want to go out with your daughter. I don't think I had the proper mentality for the game."

**113**

Aggressiveness is a must for the athlete. Too much aggressiveness, however, is dangerous. Yet we see excessive and inappropriate aggression everywhere in sports these days.

Today, it's commonplace to charge the mound when a pitcher throws at you or attack a player when they've fouled you too hard. While nothing justifies throwing at a player or committing "hard fouls," fighting fire with fire is equally unjustified. Years ago the batter would dust himself off and attempt to answer the pitcher's aggression with a line drive up the middle (or even better, a home run). Similarly, the basketball player's response would be to increase his or her effort to help put the game away.

But today charging the mound and "hard fouls" are the "macho" thing to do. And it is this kind of "sportsmanship" that is filtering down to the high schools, junior highs, and even our playgrounds.

## Athletes and Aggression: Some Alarming Stats

Athletes, unable or unwilling to leave their aggressiveness on the field, make the headlines almost daily. The April 16, 1992, issue of *USA Today* carried a scorecard of athletes who had serious difficulties handling themselves off the playing field:

| | |
|---|---|
| 1990 | Rape alleged to 3 Washington Capitals police investigation, not charged |
| 1992 | Mike Tyson rape trial convicted, serving prison term |
| 1992 | David Cone alleged sexual harassment civil suit |
| 1992 | 3 New York Mets alleged rape police investigation, not charged |
| 1992 | 15 Cincinnati Bengals alleged gang rape civil suit |
| 1992 | Trevor Berbick rape trial convicted, sentence pending |

This list serves as a grim reminder that certain tendencies must be left on the playing field. That different rules and boundaries exist in the real world and that the athlete needs to play by those rules.

## Athletes and Rape

*You seem like you're protected. You can do anything you want, and most athletes, by the time they get into prime-time, feel that they are above the law, that whatever they do, their coach will pull it out...or that someone in high power will cover up anything you do.*

- convicted rapist and ex-University of Oklahoma football player Nigel Clay, in a prison interview with Geraldo Rivera

When it comes to playing by the rules governing aggressive behavior, perhaps no area requires more attention than that of the relationship between male athletes and the women around them.

Studies show that the incidence of rape among college athletes is higher than the general student population. What does that say about how these athletes view women?

Some argue that what it says is merely an extension of society's attitudes—the same society that used to believe (and sometimes still does) that the crime of rape has something to do with sex—and that men rape because they've somehow been "enticed" or "led on" to the point where they can't control their passions.

The reality of rape is that it's a violent assault, with the penis being used as a weapon. Men don't rape because they want sexual release. There are easier ways of getting that. Men rape because they want to feel the sense of power it brings them. To say that rape is a result of passion getting out of hand is to say that a man cannot control his behavior. That is simply not true.

In an article written for the November 1992 issue of *Athletic Management* magazine, authors Timothy Marchell, James Hofher, Dr. Andrea Parrot, and Nina Cumming state that there appear to be three reasons why athletes are involved in a disproportionate number of reported sexual assaults on college campuses:

1) *Peer Pressure*

When groups of boys or men get together, they interact differently than groups of women do. The peer pressure can be more intense. When sexual situations are involved, that peer pressure can build dangerously. It can even keep individuals from doing what they know to be morally right.

## 2) *Spill-over Aggression*

Sometimes the aggression learned on the playing field carries over to relationships. An athlete gets used to viewing his opponents as adversaries. When he starts thinking of the male/female relationship as an adversarial one, that's when trouble arises.

The language of sports can further blur the lines between sex and athletic competition: Men talk about "scoring," "getting to third base," and "going all the way" as if they were in a game, not a relationship.

## 3) *Special Treatment*

The special treatment given to star athletes sometimes makes them feel like they can do whatever they want and get away with it. Special treatment can make an athlete feel like he is "entitled" to sex when and where (and with whom) he feels like it.

Nor is it just college and professional athletes who demonstrate these kinds of negative attitudes toward women. The community of Lakewood, California, was scandalized after seven girls filed complaints against members of the "Spur Posse"—a group of 20-30 young men at Lakewood High who took pride in a competition in which they scored points each time they had a sexual conquest. (One 19-year-old bragged that he was the highest scorer, with 66 points.)

At some colleges and universities, programs have been designed to educate student-athletes about what sexual assault is and how to avoid it. These programs help student-athletes examine the issues of sex, power, and communication. They learn, for example, that men look at aggression differently than women. Men typically view aggression as legitimate and "natural." Providing it stays within the rules of the sport.

They learn, too, that men and women sometimes have different rules when it comes to dating and other interactions. A woman might believe that it is okay to engage in heavy petting on a date without having to have sex; a man might think that heavy petting means sex is going to follow. When it doesn't, he may get angry at the woman for not "playing by the rules."

Ironically, in many instances of date rape, the man never even has a clue that anything went wrong. To the woman, the date was a nightmare; to the man, it was a good time. This shows the gap that can exist when men and women don't effectively communicate and understand one another's expectations and needs.

## Athletes and Domestic Violence

*"I knew he beat her," said a prominent agent in the same social loop. "It was common knowledge. A lot of his friends knew it...they all tried to keep it quiet, just like Magic's womanizing. In the small circle these athletes socialized in, people just didn't ever go public with this information. They protected him."*

- from an article on O.J. Simpson in a July 1994 issue of *Sports Illustrated*

Does being an athlete mean you are more likely than the average person to beat your spouse? Some people say yes, others disagree. Mariah Burton Nelson, a former athlete herself, says she believes there is a correlation between sports and violence against women. In discussing the O.J. Simpson case, Nelson says, "O.J. was raised in a sports culture that taught him to denigrate women...he learned the female role is to cheer men and be sexually available to men."

But Gene Upshaw, the NFL Players Association executive director, says that athletes are not necessarily more violent than non-athletes—it's just their celebrity that makes their bad behavior more noticeable. "Violent sports don't cause violent homes," Upshaw said. "It's not football that makes men hit women. The real culprit is a culture that tolerates such violence, allowing people to turn their heads and look away."

I don't believe being an athlete automatically makes you more likely to be violent. What I believe is that if you already have the traits of a violent personality, being an athlete can make it harder for you to overcome those tendencies.

Let's look at some of the elements common to the sports world that can either encourage violence or make it harder for violent individuals to recognize their problem and get help.

**Special Treatment**

When you have people always telling you how wonderful you are, or letting you off the hook when you do something wrong, it makes it harder for you to have a true picture of yourself. One of the characteristics of batterers is their refusal to see themselves for what they really are, and their refusal to see what they're doing as wrong.

**Terminal Adolescence**

Part of the adolescent response to things that go wrong is to refuse to take responsibility. Psychologist Ellen Ledley noted that Simpson's well-publicized comments about his marriage showed complete denial that any problem existed. She went on to state, "The problem with most men who batter is that they use denial, avoidance, minimizing, that it's just between us."

**Impulsiveness**

Some experts said that O.J. Simpson's flight from justice suggested that he is an impulsive personality—in other words, he *reacts* instead of *acts*. Impulsiveness is a trait that many athletes have. It helps them to quickly respond to things that happen on the field, and, in that sense, it's a valuable trait. Unfortunately, impulsiveness is also a trait found in batterers. When things start going wrong in their lives, they don't act to make them better. Instead, they let the pressure build until they just explode—in other words, a *re*action.

**Difficulty in Maintaining Relationships**

In the upcoming chapter on relationships, I discuss some of the challenges athletes may experience when it comes to maintaining a successful relationship with the opposite sex. Poor communication skills, intensity, ego problems...these are all barriers athletes sometimes face. They are also traits that are common in batterers. Batterers often strike out because they lack the communication skills to otherwise resolve their problems. Batterers also struggle with low self-esteem. For example, the fact that O.J.'s post-sports career didn't bring him the same kind of adulation football did may have caused his self-esteem to drop. Not being able to keep his marriage together may also have caused O.J. to feel less than successful. All these factors could have contributed to the battering syndrome.

## Aggression vs. Assertion

In the real world, one doesn't deal with an opponent by tackling, punching, or yelling. Unfortunately, too many athletes resort to violence as a form of communication. Robert Lipsyte, a columnist for *The New York Times*, has said, "This is how we condition our sports heroes and, by extension, so many political and business leaders brought up on the varsity syndrome of winner take all, winning at any cost, violence as a tool, aggression as a mark of masculinity."

Aggression in sporting events is not only normal, but it is supported by athletes, coaches, and fans. In the real world, however, aggression must become assertion. What's the difference? I offer the following illustration:

You're sitting in a restaurant, ready to order, but the waitress keeps walking by you. If you react aggressively, you might yell at the waitress, tell her she's stupid, and quite possibly storm out of the restaurant without even ordering. If, however, you react assertively, you'd calmly, but firmly, flag the waitress down and place an order. (Thirdly, if you were completely non-assertive, you'd just sit there, fuming, until the waitress finally appeared.)

The assertive person speaks up for what he or she wants. Speaking up, though, doesn't involve yelling or hitting or throwing a tantrum. It means being firm, in control. Everyone needs assertiveness in their life. The challenge athletes face is how to recognize the difference between assertiveness and aggression; learning how to turn the aggressiveness that serves them so well on the field into the assertiveness that will serve them equally well off the field.

## Practice Time

Many times, people resort to aggressive behavior because they have problems communicating any other way. The better you can become at other methods of communication, the less likely you will be to lash out with aggression. Here are some suggestions for improving your communication skills:

• participate in classes and/or seminars on communication skills (these are frequently offered as part of high school and college curricula, and as business workshops)

• learn about the issue of sexual assault (you can obtain information from your local rape crisis center or most libraries)

• carefully read Chapters 28 and 29 of this book, dealing with communication skills, and complete the exercises at the end of those chapters

# PART THREE

# After the Game:
# Transitioning From Sports to Life

# 19
# WHEN THE CHEERING STOPS

## The Game Plan

In this chapter, I will talk about:

- dealing with the emotions that are triggered by the end of your playing days
- the ways in which people respond to change
- how to manage change
- what sports teach you about the transition game
- the seven stages of transition
- "training down" for the next stage in your life

*One life had ended, and another had not yet quite begun. For some years I had known this moment would come, but now it was here in earnest. I had to negotiate the middle passage between the old and the new. Quite consciously, I gave myself a period of about three months simply to think about the past and about the future. At this crucial point in my life, I did not want to make any major mistakes.*

*Looking back on that period, I see only one thing clearly; that it seemed to me quite possibly a developing crisis. I felt a subtle but pervasive dissatisfaction with my life up to that point, and a deep confusion about what the rest of it would, and should, look like.*

*- Arthur Ashe, Days of Grace*

When the cheering stops, the silence can be deadly.

After children leave the nest, parents sometimes sit in the silence of their empty house and wonder what they're going to do with the rest of their lives. A retiree asks the same question at 65. For the athlete, that question may come at 30, 20, or 16.

"What am I going to do with the rest of my life?" is never an easy question. If sports is the end all of your life, it can be even harder to answer. Why? Because it raises other questions. Issues the athlete may either have denied, been unaware of, or, simply been unable to handle. Questions like: "What skills do I have beyond my athletic abilities?" "Can I get a real job?" "How do I deal with my feelings about these changes?" For the athlete who built (or dreamed of building) a life around sports, the end of the dream signals that it's time to move on.

When the cheering stops, the silence that remains affects each athlete differently. Some, like Bill Bradley, wake up to their new lives with a minimum of discomfort. Others find the silence confusing, even frightening. One former athlete likened it to "being dipped into hell." Perhaps the scariest thought of all is that your athletic years have been the high point of your life and everything else will be anticlimactic.

For me, the end of my athletic career came suddenly. After eating, drinking, and sleeping basketball for 14 years, it was over. Though drafted by the Philadelphia Warriors after college, something kept me from accepting. Looking back, I think I feared how much sports controlled me and I wanted to make the break.

It wasn't a clean break. I spent the season following my last college game as a graduate student who also assisted with the freshman and varsity teams. I was still part of the sport but definitely out of the limelight. My glory days were over. I remember as if it was last week, nothing felt real. Things were vague and unfamiliar. It was not a good time. Painful. I know now that I was in mourning. It took several years before I would heal. In some ways, I'm still healing.

There is nothing unusual about the struggles young people face as they seek direction in life. For former athletes, however, the struggle can seem harder because they've lost the major focus of their lives.

No matter how competent you are on the playing field, once you move off the field you may feel unprepared and unappreciated. Whatever success you find in the real world, it may never match the excitement, the enthusiasm, or the camaraderie of the game.

Any ending, whether created by the loss of a job, a relationship, or the end of one's playing days, triggers deep feelings and emotions. A person must deal with the end to break off from it and start anew. Failure to deal with this loss can keep you attached to the past with little or no energy to concentrate on the present.

Athletes who fail to adjust to the demands of life off the field live with one foot in the athletic world and one foot in the real world. Jim Parker, for example, spent 11 years as an offensive guard with the Baltimore Colts. After his retirement, Parker said that before every Colts game he would have such a strong physical reaction that he'd need to leave his convenience store and drive around Baltimore until he let off the tension. He just couldn't accept that the game was over for him.

If you tie your identity and self-esteem to your sports performance, then thinking of life off-the-field can lead you to ask, "How do I live—what sort of person am I—without the attention, the adulation, and the focus my ability to make touchdowns or serve aces affords?"

It doesn't have to be that way, though. When the cheering stops, the silence can be a time of peace and reflection. It can be a time of purpose. A time to think, as Arthur Ashe did, about the past and plan for the future. A "time-out" to recognize that your life is changing and to start work on your new life.

## Responding to Change

*I got to the top very quickly, and stayed there seven or eight years, but my heart said, "Listen, it's time to change, to adapt, to smooth some edges." I felt like that's what I was doing when I took a step back, but I got stubborn. I wasn't addressing the real problems. I said, "You've been winning too long to change now," and I wasn't able to adjust...*
- John McEnroe, speaking of his tennis career

In the real world, change is constant. People under the age of 35, for example, change jobs an average of once every year and a half. These same individuals will have an estimated three to five careers in a lifetime.

Technology evolves as well. Twenty-five years ago, computers were expensive, bulky machines that few people had even seen, let alone worked on. Today, the computer is integral to our lives. It has been said that had the automobile industry made the same kind of advances the computer industry has, a Rolls Royce would cost $2.98, get 20,000 miles to a gallon—and everyone would own one.

Society, too, changes. Events in Eastern Europe and the former Soviet Union are redefining global politics even as the United States struggles to keep up with a far larger and diverse society than our founding fathers ever anticipated.

As the world moves ever faster, we keep trying to slow it down. As John McEnroe discovered, resisting change is human nature. Nevertheless, change is a necessary part of being. When we cease to change—to grow, develop, experience—we might as well cease to exist.

The end of your playing days means the beginning of a new chapter in your life—a chapter in which you must:

- Prepare to make a significant adjustment
- Know that this adjustment means making changes
- Have the courage to fight through the emotions these changes may bring

These changes may not be easy. Change, whether positive or negative, is one of the most stressful things that can occur in your life. It affects both your physical and mental well-being.

Some are better than others in handling change. To get an idea of how flexible you are when it comes to change, complete the following exercise. Circle the number that best corresponds to your attitude regarding the two opposing statements.

| | | |
|---|---|---|
| I view any change as an opportunity, not a threat. | 5 4 3 2 1 | I reject all change as a personal threat. |
| If my sport should introduce new techniques or equipment for me to use, I would be delighted. | 5 4 3 2 1 | If forced to learn how to use new techniques or equipment, I would be openly hostile. |

| A reorganization of my athletic department would be welcome. | 5 4 3 2 1 | I would hate any form of reorganization; I like things stable. |
|---|---|---|
| I have an excellent coach, but a change would not bother me. | 5 4 3 2 1 | I have an excellent coach; a change would devastate me. |
| New assignments and responsibilities motivate me. | 5 4 3 2 1 | New assignments and responsibilities do not motivate me. |
| All of the social and political changes taking place today are exciting to me. | 5 4 3 2 1 | I wish I had lived 100 years ago. |
| Predictability is dull. | 5 4 3 2 1 | Predictability is great! |
| The possibility of change intrigues me. | 5 4 3 2 1 | The possibility of change scares me. |
| I have confidence that I can quickly change my behavior to fit any situation. | 5 4 3 2 1 | It is almost impossible for me to change my behavior. |
| I can change my goals and lifestyle quickly. | 5 4 3 2 1 | My goals and dreams are imbedded in cement. |

TOTAL: _____

*If you scored above 25, you appear to have a positive, flexible attitude toward change. You should handle future changes ably. A score below 25, however, indicates that you have less flexibility than you may need to cope well with change.*

In general, people tend to respond to change to in one of four ways. See if you can recognize yourself in any of the following examples:

1) *The Maintainer*

The maintainers want things to stay the same. They'll do anything to preserve the illusion that nothing has changed. In their minds, they're still young, healthy, and gifted. This strategy is seen not only in the significant number of professional athletes who want to extend their careers beyond reasonable limits, but also in the fanatics who "play" their sport five nights a week to the exclusion of other activities.

Maintainers often idealize the past as a refuge from the harshness of the real world. In the past, everything was "perfect." These people are often passive in their approach to life and unlikely to take the opportunity to alter existing behavior, beliefs, or values.

2) *The Rebel*

Rebels respond to change by suddenly rejecting former values and beliefs. Their revolt may be against familiar people, places, ideas, or objects. Marvin Cobb, who used to play for the Detroit Lions and is now an administrator at the University of Southern California, had a rebellious response to retirement. Marvin didn't watch a football game for six years after his release, so great was his pain and anguish.

The rebellious person is often angry and aggressive. Not only do they reject the past, but they don't see much happiness for the future.

3) *The Escape Artist*

Others escape from change. Escaping is a way of evading the present pain by turning to numbing chemicals or behaviors. Increased use of alcohol, drugs, sleep, food, or other addictive patterns are all methods of escape. Maury Wills followed a successful career with the Los Angeles Dodgers and an unsuccessful stint as manager of the Seattle Mariners with a three-and-a-half year drug binge. Speaking of his experience, Wills said: "Some players, after their career, go on to have nice, normal, productive lives, but a lot of us fall prey to disaster, because [life after baseball] is the [real] big leagues."

Escape artists are looking for someone else to come in and

take control. Yet when someone suggests a solution to their problems, it's usually resented. In order to break this pattern, the escape artist needs to develop the self-control and self-discipline necessary to deal with reality.

4) *The Pacesetter*

"When life gives you lemons, make lemonade!" That's the strategy pacesetters use. This approach requires an openness to change and loss. One must view change as an opportunity to grow.

Few people offer a better example of this attitude than former major league pitcher Dave Dravecky. After being treated for cancer in his pitching arm, Dravecky returned to the mound in triumph. After a third tumor was discovered, however, he knew there would be no more comebacks. Dravecky ended up losing his arm to cancer.

Instead of sitting around moaning about his misfortune, Dravecky, a deeply religious man, hit the road as a motivational speaker, sharing his faith and helping others through their troubles. Dave Dravecky saw the big picture. And baseball didn't take up the whole frame. "When your eye is only on eternity," he said, "you can handle what happens in the present."

## Managing Change

If you found that, when it comes to dealing with change, you are a maintainer, a rebel, or an escape artist, don't worry. It *is* possible to learn how to manage change. Here are some ways to make the process easier:

• *Deal directly with your problems.*

You did not achieve athletic success by avoiding or denying your weaknesses. If you couldn't hit a curveball, you went to the batting cage. If you kept slicing your drives off the tee, you adjusted your swing and practiced till you got it right. You improved your game by confronting your problems, not ignoring them.

• *Don't forget that change involves real loss.*

That last whistle ends much more than your athletic career.

It sounds the loss of friends, structure, and, possibly, a sense of who you are. It also signals a process as natural as the healing of a physical wound. Trust nature to do the healing. Know that the anger, pain, sadness, and grieving will pass.

• *Talk about your feelings.*

Share your thoughts with your friends and family. Listen to their feelings and suggestions. This helps make you sensitive to your reactions to the changes in your life. Their honest and objective feedback will aid you in coping.

• *Establish a support group.*

You've had the encouragement and support of your teammates to get you through tough times in the past. You need to create a new team to help you through the changes involved in stepping off the field and moving on to the next chapter of your life.

• *Recognize that depression is often part of change.*

We will discuss depression in depth later in this section, but it is important to understand at the outset that depression is your body's attempt to get your attention. It's a wake-up call informing you that you are experiencing difficulty in building your new life.

• *Don't try to fight change.*

Accept the fact that a transition is taking place. Get past the point of fighting it so you can attend to what needs to be done. As a psychologist, I've been asked many times if people really change. The answer to that is, of course, yes. People change when they stop avoiding or denying the truth and use the energy they've been wasting on defensive mechanisms to move forward. For example, if your coach tells you that your form is inhibiting your efficiency and effectiveness and you refuse to accept this truth, you will not improve. If, however, you take the energy you would have burned up resisting the coach and apply it to learning a better way of shooting that free throw or jumping that hurdle, your performance will improve.

Finally, you need to remember two things regarding change. One, you'll never change unless *you* want to. The dissatisfaction or desire of others may start the change process, but it can't sustain it. Two, remember to be realistic when it comes to change. Events may change overnight, but people don't. One of the main reasons people give up is because they try to do too much too soon. They try to win the match instead of the point, and they find themselves overwhelmed. When you face change one day at a time, one step at a time, you build the foundations that help you move on to the opportunities that lie ahead.

## Moving On

*I had a neat, privileged life. I was spared some of the aggravation of being a teenager, made great money, girls screamed. But after the series folded, it was like I was handed the bill for all the privileges I had enjoyed.*
- Paul Petersen, one-time heartthrob Jeff Stone of "The Donna Reed Show"

*The hardest thing for an athlete to do is to know when to quit. When do you let go of the thing that has shaped your entire life?*
-Isiah Thomas

*The one thing that tells you most about a person is the ability to make transitions.*
- Jerry West, general manager of the Los Angeles Lakers

Basketball coaches often talk about the transition game. They know that a team's ability to go from offense to defense after a turnover or missed shot has a lot do with winning games and championships. The transition game requires players to let go of their mistakes, disappointments, or even celebrations and hustle back down the court.

When you step off the field, you sometimes have to replace the self-confidence that sports gives you. It's a new kind of "transition game." It can be frustrating. As Paul Petersen mentioned, being a star at a young age kept him from experiencing some of the frustrations of a typical teenager. Still, we mature and establish our identities by overcoming those universal teenage aggravations. People who are spared aren't being done any favors.

When your self-definition comes through sports and you stop playing, you may feel that you've lost your identity. By establishing confidence in yourself as an individual apart from athletics, you can help to redefine that identity.

## Seven Stages of Transition

Life's transitional periods are seldom easy. They mark a time when you are breaking with the comfort of the known and entering the discomfort of the unknown. I've found that major transitions usually involve seven stages:

1) *Numbness*
Numbness is when nothing feels real to you. You're just going through the motions.

2) *Denial*
You convince yourself you can still play, despite the fact that (choose one):
• you've received a career-ending injury
• no one has drafted you or offered you a scholarship
• you're getting too old to keep up with the youngsters

Denial can also occur after you leave the game. As one former athlete stated: "Professional football players feel they are superior beings and that when the time comes to retire, they will deal with it. But as I found out, you can't prepare yourself enough...I was in a state of denial. I thought I could make the jump from sports to society with no problems. But my beliefs started to break up after about six months."

3) *Self-doubt and/or Depression*
You feel you'll never be able to do anything as well (or find anything as exciting) as sports.

4) *Acceptance*
You accept that your playing days are over and begin to look forward to the next phase of your life.

5) *Testing*

You try out new behaviors and lifestyles. This can be a positive or negative experience, depending on how well you've handled the other stages of transition.

6) *Search for Meaning*

You experience a gradual shift toward understanding, when you ask: "Is this right for me?" "Have I found my new niche?"

7) *Internalization*

Your new life becomes a significant part of you. It feels right and your self-esteem is restored.

It may take you anywhere from several weeks to several years to move through all of these transition stages. Part of the difficulty is that, for an athlete, the transition from playing to not playing means letting go of the dream. It is hard to let go of the dream you've probably cherished for years. But whether you are a recreational or an elite athlete, you need to learn how to let go and move on. Gracefully. It's something few athletes know how to do. Magic Johnson said he was quitting but couldn't. His first departure from basketball was untimely but poignant. His second was messy and painful.

While it is important to have and to follow dreams, recognizing when the dream has ended is equally important. The transition period that occurs when you let go of your dreams of athletic achievement can also be known by another term: training down.

For some athletes, the shock of retiring from formal competition is so great that it produces post-traumatic stress symptoms. Bruce Ogilvie, a sports psychologist in San Jose, California, has worked with a number of athletes who "are very terrified, at times suicidal, because their careers are over."

Reportedly, former East German athletes used to train down from elite competition both physically and emotionally. Any athlete, however, who wants to let go of an unachieved goal or dream and move on to new ones may find the training down process a helpful one.

Training down involves weaning yourself away from your dependency on sports. It means gradually cutting your physical workouts to a level that can be comfortably maintained for general fitness purposes. It means, too, reducing your emotional dependency on sports. You hear professional athletes talk about knowing it's time to quit when they no longer feel the intensity or drive that they used to. In a sense, that's their mind's way of beginning the separation process.

Tim Burke's separation from baseball began in 1991, the day before his young adopted daughter's heart surgery. Burke discovered the Montreal Expos had just traded him to the New York Mets—and he would have to leave soon after the operation was over. It would be more than a month before the family could be together again. "It was the first time in my life that I found myself out on the mound not concentrating at all," Burke said. Even though baseball had been *"beyond a dream"* for Burke, he found himself rethinking his priorities. At spring training in 1993, worried about the effects of his absences on his wife and children, Burke discovered "my heart and passion weren't on the ballfield. They were with my family." So he retired from the game that meant so much to him.

During the transition period, it is important to remember that your life is not over, even if it feels like it is. Even though Tim Burke knew he'd made the right decision, it was still a difficult one. He described the long drive home: "I'm looking in the rearview mirror and seeing the ballpark getting smaller and smaller. It was a perfect picture of how baseball was going to be in my life."

When Ted Danson left the TV show "Cheers"—a show he'd spent the major part of his adult life working on—he likened it to diving off the high dive:

> ... I feel like I'm on kind of a high board—a high diving board, about to spring into I don't know what. A new, scary place. And I'm excited about diving into this new, scary place. I don't know what's waiting for me, maybe a big old belly-flop... I want to jump into this void and scare the hell out of myself.

Transitions, change—they're all a little scary. But then, so are rollercoaster rides. Don't be afraid to be afraid. The fear is part of the thrill.

## Practice Time

To better understand your feelings about change and how you can put those feelings to positive use, undertake the following exercise:

- For two weeks, carry a notebook with you. Each day, write down the following:
    - every negative emotion you feel
    - what caused it
    - what, if anything, you did about it
    - every positive emotion you feel
    - what caused it
    - what you did to increase or diminish the positive feelings

- At the end of each day, study the notes you have made. What can you learn from them? (The point is to become more conscious of what you feel and how you react to those feelings.)

- Try to become more adaptable to change by incorporating more change in your life. Each week, try something new. Suggestions:
    - Try a new food (such as Kiwi, tofu, eggplant, etc.)
    - Read a book you wouldn't ordinarily read
    - Take a different route home from school or work

- Pick something in your life that you need to change, or that you need to do in order to better adapt to change. List specific steps you will do in order to achieve that change.
    Examples:
    Since I didn't get the sports scholarship I was hoping for, I need to find some other ways to help finance my schooling. To do this, I will:
    - Talk to a counselor about other financial aid options
    - Get information about on-campus jobs for when school starts
    - Get a part-time or summer job that will help me save money now

- Now that my athletic career is over, I need to get serious about looking for another job. To do this, I will:
    - Write my résumé
    - Send out five résumés per week
    - Try to set up three interviews per week
    - Network with at least two people per week

# 20
# MAKING THE TRANSITION
## Building Your Life Skills

*Many are anxious to improve their circumstances but are unwilling to improve themselves; they therefore remain bound.*
- James Allen, American novelist

*He who is not prepared today will be less so tomorrow.*
- Ovid, Roman poet

When I was in my early 40s, I got "serious" about tennis and entered a local tournament. My opponent was an older, overweight stockbroker who told me that he had played quite a bit throughout his life. Nevertheless, I figured I'd have little difficulty beating him, considering the shape he was in.

Wrong! I may have been in better shape, but my opponent had better skills. His skill level more than compensated for his lack of conditioning. This just goes to show that you should never underestimate the power of building a solid foundation of skills.

Just as building your athletic skills can help you become a successful athlete, building your "life skills" can help you be more successful at life. Life skills do not consist of merely getting a degree from high school or college. Life skills go beyond mere learning. I got my degree from a prominent university, but my life was so structured by my scholarship requirements and athletics that I had little energy left for real learning, as opposed to just completing assignments.

Life skills are what develop you as a person. That is the purpose of this section: to review those basic skills that will help you develop academically, socially, emotionally, physically, and spiritually.

Your goal is to prepare yourself for life after sports. If you are a student athlete, one way you can do this is to be a part of your school "community," that is, being more than just a campus jock. In college, especially, the growth process that occurs is very important. Involvement in athletics should not preclude opportunities for growth in other areas.

Like me, you may think that you don't have the time or energy to do much more than concentrate on your sport. It's important, though, to find the time.

Even professional sports are beginning to recognize the need for athletes to learn the skills that will help prepare them for life in—and out of—the big leagues. Baseball, for example, has developed a Rookie Career Development program. The goal is to help rookies make the transition in a variety of areas. Some of the things they learn about include financial planning, tax preparation, the media, and the celebrity experience. (The NBA offers a similar program for rookies, which I've been fortunate to be a part of.)

Former San Francisco 49ers coach Bill Walsh has talked about the need for learning skills that will help you in any situation you may find yourself. He said, "Making judgments under severe stress is the most difficult thing there is. The more preparation you have prior to the conflict…the better off you will be."

Whether your immediate future is in professional sports, further education, or some other line of work, you need to develop those skills and abilities that will interest employers and admission officers. You also need to develop the qualities that will enable you to enjoy satisfying relationships—both with yourself and with others.

Just because you're a good athlete doesn't mean you carry that same confidence off the field. Building your life skills will gain you that confidence. It will help you realize that you're a talented individual who has demonstrated a variety of inner resources in your sports career—resources that you can transfer to other fields of interest.

This section will help you to recognize the skills you already have, as well as teach you the basics of some new skills.

## Skill-Building Techniques

As you read each chapter, keep in mind the following general skill-building strategies and use these techniques anytime you learn a new skill:

- Ask for feedback and advice. This can keep you from developing bad habits.

- Find role models. Good teachers produce good students.

- Seek to coach yourself, as well. In other words, do the things that coaches do: use good management techniques, set reachable goals, give feedback, offer encouragement and support.

- Practice. Publilius Syrus, the Latin writer, said, "Practice is the best of all instructors." Place yourself in situations where you have to practice what you learn.

Transition follows any ending, whether it's the end of a game, a season, or a career. For some, the end of their athletic dream may come in high school or college. For others, it won't come until later. Regardless of when or how your game finally ends, making the transition from a world focused on sports to a world focused on something else can be challenging.

In the upcoming chapters, you will be learning more about:

- the transition that occurs when your playing days end
- the skills that will help you both during and after the transition

Hopefully, the things you learn here will help you to successfully face any of the transitions that may occur in your life.

# 21
# SCOUTING YOURSELF
## Taking Stock of Who You Are

### The Game Plan

In this chapter I will talk about:

- the danger of basing your identity on your athletic achievements
- how to determine if too much of your identity is centered on sports
- getting to know the real "you"

*The unexamined life is not worth living.*
- Socrates

*He who knows another is wise; he who knows himself is enlightened.*
- Lao Tzu

Draw a circle. This circle represents you. Within that circle, draw another circle that represents your athletic "self." The size of the second circle should reflect how important sports is in your life as this point in time.

How big is the second circle, in comparison to the first? Does it take up all of the first circle? Half of it? Only a small portion?

The more you base your identity on sports, the harder the transition to life off the field will be. Finding the desire or the ability to learn new skills and discover new interests will prove difficult as well. That's why the first "life skill" we'll talk about is scouting yourself—getting to know yourself, your talents, skills, strengths, and limitations.

Scouting yourself requires you to do two things:

- determine how much of your identity is centered on sports
- get to know the "you" that exists apart from sports

## The Athletic Identity

*The athletes who succeed in making college teams have the high school experience duplicated on a grander scale. The few who excel on university teams find that admiration comes then, not from high school friends and adult family friends, but from the national press and from adults they have never met. They begin to see that they can make a good living simply by playing the sport. Self-definition again comes from external sources, not from within. While their physical skill lasts, professional athletes are celebrities—fondled and excused, praised and believed. Only toward the end of their careers do the stars realize that their sense of identity is insufficient.*
- Bill Bradley, *Life on the Run*

*Once I'd had so many dreams and goals; now there was a vacuum. Ever since I was a child, my identity and self-esteem had come from my performance on and around the court. I had to find other outlets.*
- Tracy Austin

*Despite his enormous success, Simpson always needed this constant reassurance of others, the validation of cheering crowds. He could recognize himself only in the mirror held up by others.*
- "Simpson and Sudden Death," *U.S. News and World Report*

Part of being an athlete is being competitive. Unfortunately, very competitive people often attach large portions of their identity and self-worth to achieving success through certain activities. For the athlete, that activity is sports.

Many athletes have said that the hardest thing to adjust to once their playing days end isn't the loss of money or the need to find a new career direction. It's the loss of identity. Suddenly, they're someone who "used to be" somebody important.

*Am I Someone Who...*

Ask yourself the following "Am I someone who...?" questions and answer each yes or no.

*... Has had a long period of athletic success?*

My success on the basketball court began at an early age and continued on through high school and college. After all those years, seeing myself as successful at anything else took work.

*... Has received a lot of public acclaim?*

I received praise, recognition, and publicity for my sports accomplishments—including a front-page, full-length picture in the calendar section of the *San Francisco Examiner* with the caption, "The Greatest Thing Since Mickey Mouse." I don't know if public acclaim became an addiction, but it left its mark on my life. To this day, a need for recognition and appreciation, coupled with a strong desire to please people, shapes me.

*... Is economically dependent on sports?*

When you're paid for it (either with a scholarship or cash), you view sports differently. I was economically dependent on basketball. Stanford "paid" me a full scholarship to play, thus, defining me as an athlete more than a scholar.

*... Has unclear non-sports career goals?*

I started college as a pre-med student but couldn't handle the math and chemistry. From there I changed my major four or five times and finally ended up with a degree that in no way reflected my interest or talents.

*... Has a strong masculine identity?*

Sports seems central to the definition of manhood in our society. My only clue to what it meant to be a man came from the athletic field. Eventually, I developed a softer side (the nurturing side) by entering professions that gave me permission to care for other people the way I secretly wanted them to care for me.

*... Has a low social class identity?*

Blue collar values and athletics go hand in hand. Although my father was a dentist who made a better-than-average living, he was also a German Jew, not the best thing to be in the 1940s and '50s. We lived modestly; whether because my parents were from the depression era or for other reasons, I'm not sure. Regardless, I *felt* poor compared to our less frugal neighbors.

*... Has few non-sports achievements or recognition?*

I served on the student council and worked on the school newspaper (in high school), but never threw myself into these activities as I did into sports. I did not develop other interests (drama, scouting, music, etc.) nor nurture other skills, or free my identity from the overbearing ties of athletic accomplishments until many, many years after my playing days ended.

*... Has little capacity for intimacy?*

Sports participation hampers successful intimate relationships which can support you through difficulties during the transition period. Just look at the divorce rate among professional athletes.

The intimacy level in my first marriage was very low. The dinner table was a refueling station for my body. For my wife, however, it was a place to socialize. We were at cross-purposes and neither one of us gained much from what little interaction could take place between mouthfuls of "fuel."

*... Began sports training at an early age?*

The earlier you begin, the more your athletic identity engulfs your total identity.

*...Has little social interaction with family, non-athletic peers, and ethnic/religious groups?*

Interaction with these groups provides you with a sense of belonging and identity that is separate from the playing field. They give you more balance in your life.

If you answered yes to more than four of these questions, then you need to work on establishing an identity that is not based on your sports accomplishments. Without a strong identity apart from your sports "self," the transition from the sports world to real world will be even harder.

I am indebted to Dr. David Epperson, a colleague and former teammate of mine, for these variables impacting athletic identity. Dave developed them in a matter of minutes after reading my initial draft of this chapter. When I asked him how he was able to come up with these points so quickly, Dave said, "Oh, that was easy! I just contrasted your life with mine."

## Getting to Know You

One of the things Philadelphia 76ers coach John Lucas learned as he struggled to overcome his alcohol and drug addiction was that his recovery depended on finding out who he really was. All his life he defined himself through sports, basing his self-esteem on how well he performed as an athlete. Through the process of recovery, Lucas discovered himself.

"Basketball and tennis are what I did; this is who I am," Lucas says. "My name is John, and I'm a grateful addict-alcoholic... What I thought was the worst possible deal in life has turned out to be the best gift I've been given. My addiction carried me past my sports life. It gave me my best trophy. It gave me John Lucas."

Getting to know yourself—your good points as well as bad—is part of the process of maturing as a human being. We might call it a "life assignment" as its completion is necessary to successfully compete in the bigger game of life. Knowing yourself is also a lifelong assignment because there are always new things to learn and discover about yourself as you go through life.

The act of self-discovery is not necessarily an easy one. Neither is it particularly mystical or mysterious. Sitting in a dark room, burning incense, and making funny noises is not required (although you can, if you want). What is required, what you absolutely *must* do is question, observe, reflect, and analyze.

The following questions will help you assess your identity at this time in your life. Take your time in answering them and try to give several answers for each. Write them down or record them for later review.

1) What are the things that you most like to do, or the activities that have the most meaning for you?
2) How often do you do the above activities?
3) Does anything prevent you from doing the things you value as frequently as you'd like? If so, what?
4) What are some specific actions you can take to increase the amount of meaningful activity in your life?

5)  Who are you?  Try completing the sentence, "I am...," 20 different ways, quickly writing down the words or phrases that immediately occur to you.
6)  What does this list tell you about how you view yourself?

Here are some further suggestions for learning more about yourself:

• *Keep a journal.*
A journal is a written record of what you do, why you do it, and what the results of your activities are.  It includes your emotions: doubts, joys, fears, and hopes.  A journal is an important tool for increasing your personal and professional growth.  It also helps you to see yourself objectively. When we look at our lives on paper, it's easier to see our mistakes and to be honest with ourselves.

• *Spend time alone.*
This is not as easy a suggestion as you might think.  How often do you turn off the television, put away the book, and remove yourself from the distraction and demands of other people?  Being alone with your thoughts  can be a powerful tool in your search to discover what you want to be and have and do after sports.

• *Note the things that make you unique.*
Someone once mentioned to me that self-worth has a lot to do with feeling that you are unique or special in your own eyes. You gain this feeling by identifying those things you like or value about yourself.

• *Note the things that have made you happy.*
In the bestselling career book, *What Color is Your Parachute?*, Richard Nelson Bolles reports that many people who are trying to decide on a career change have never taken inventory of their past experiences, prioritizing those accomplishments that made them the happiest and most fulfilled.  Make a list of past experiences and accomplishments that have brought you joy.  Rank them in order of importance.

• *Continue to define yourself.*

Whenever someone comments about the number of different careers I've had—clergyman, coach, referee, psychologist, executive, consultant—I like to reply that it's all evolutionary. What I mean by this is that I see life as a process of evolving and unfolding, rather than a matter of simply "finding" ourselves. I have suggested that it might be helpful to try to capture, on paper, who you are and where you are going *at this time*. Be careful about making any permanent definitions, however, because that can make you resistant to change and growth. Review the list periodically, perhaps when January 1 comes each year, noting what has and has not changed and what adjustments you have made.

## Practice Time

Compile a scouting report on yourself by completing the following assignments:

• Complete some of the exercises suggested on pages 146-47 (such as setting a goal to keep a journal for one month, or to spend one hour a week alone and away from all distractions).

• Make a list of your strengths and weaknesses. Ask some friends and family members to do the same. Compare the lists to get a more accurate picture of yourself.

# 22
# BUILDING YOUR TEAM
## How to Put Together a New Support System

### The Game Plan

In this chapter, I will talk about:

- how your support team can help you make the transition from sports to the real world
- how to "recruit" your support team
- mentors: why they're one of the most critical parts of your team

*No man is wise enough by himself.*
- Titus Plautus, 200 B.C.

*What I'm trying to do is meet people on campus, you never know who down the line might help you get a job after football is all over.*
- Anton Gunn, football player and co-chairperson of South Carolina's student-athlete committee

It has been said that the whole is greater than the sum of its parts. In sports, and in life, a team is capable of far more than the mere sum of the individuals who comprise it.

Research shows that teams of 5 to 15 people, cooperating with each other and brainstorming ideas, accomplish far more than brilliant individuals working alone. No matter what it is you're trying to do, teams are the most effective way to get the job done.

As you begin this new game, it's time to assemble a new team—a network of old and new friends who can assist, support, encourage, and challenge you.

The people who make up your "team" will fill several functions. They are there to provide you with honest feedback. They can help you discover who you are. They will push you in directions you've never gone before.

**145**

So how do you go about building your new team? As an athlete, it was easy. If you played a team sport, you had a built-in support system that included your teammates, coaches, and trainers. Now you're the one responsible for putting together the team. Here are some recruiting guidelines:

• *Choose your team carefully.*

Former Dodger pitcher Joe Black said the hardest part about making the transition from baseball to a new career was accepting the fact that 85 percent of the contacts he made while playing were phonies. When President Clinton assembled his White House staff, some of the key positions went to friends he had known since childhood. Those were the people he knew he could count on. Perhaps he felt the same as Arthur Ashe, who stated in his memoir:

> I make it a point to keep in touch with friends
> from my childhood in Richmond; I cannot help
> but think that childhood friends are the bedrock
> of all one's future relationships, and that you
> move away from them at your risk. There is an
> African proverb in which I believe: Hold on to
> your friends with both hands.

• *Identify what you need from your team.*

Do you need someone who can help you pass advanced calculus? Someone who can offer job-hunting tips? Someone who shares your weird sense of humor? Some positions on your team will be long-term, others will just be temporary. Knowing what you need will help you pick the best candidates.

• *Identify which people on your "recruiting list" can meet your needs.*

Different people fill different needs. *Energizers*, for example, are those individuals with the ability to motivate you when the going gets tough. *Experts* can provide information and expertise in your field of interest. *Challengers* force you to stretch yourself. *Access providers* cut through red tape and gain you access to varied resources.

• *Recruit your team.*

When it comes to putting together your new team, asking for help can be the most difficult task of all. Some people won't have to be asked at all—they'll just be there for you no matter what. Other people will need an invitation. Invite these people to "play on your team" in a straightforward manner. Be specific about what you are doing, why, and the role you would like them to play. Offer to assist them, as well. Remember that teammates develop trust and skill by working together frequently—not by calling on each other only in emergencies.

## Mentors

*A single conversation across the table with a wise man is worth a month's study of books.*
- Chinese proverb

Since people seldom improve without role models, one of the most important slots to fill on your new team is that of "mentor." Mentors show you how things are done. They take a special interest in you, providing the encouragement you need to keep your problems and goals in perspective. Most of all, mentors give you valuable models of how to conduct yourself in the world.

Who makes a good mentor? Someone who has "been there" and can help with difficult evaluations or decisions. Someone who is sensitive, accessible, and who leads by example. If you're in school, a mentor can be an upperclassman, a teacher, or counselor. In the workplace, a mentor can be a coworker or boss.

The lucky athlete may be able to say, "My coach is my mentor," but, more often than not, coaches are more interested in you as an athlete than as a person. They tend to take a dominant, rather than supportive, position in an athlete's life—which is contrary to the concept of mentorship.

Mentorship, at its best, makes a difference. When it goes beyond the usual supportive, administrative, or tutorial function of, say, a coach, supervisor, or manager, mentorship does more than help a person learn a new skill. Rather, it focuses on the in-depth development of the individual.

Research supports the importance of mentors. Psychologist Daniel Levinson conducted a study of middle-aged men in various careers. Those surveyed emphasized the significance of mentors in the shaping of their professional lives. Women moving up the corporate ladder have often spoken of being handicapped by the lack of other women executives to serve as mentors and role models.

I can think of many instance of mentoring in my life, but two stand out. One was George "Shorty" Kellogg, the physical director at the YMCA in Long Beach, California, when I was young. Shorty taught me the joy of being part of a team and how to respect my teammates and opponents.

The second mentoring experience was more recent. Like many people of my generation, I've resisted using a computer. To be frank, they scare me. Then one day, a client sent me a MacIntosh. That was when a friend of mine (who I was then sharing an office with) decided it was high time I made my entrance into the Computer Age. Sitting by my side, offering encouragement at every step, he helped me tame the mechanical beast in front of me. There was no way I could have done it without him as a mentor.

As a champion race car driver Emerson Fittipaldi noted, success is seldom a one-person job: "I've learned you need a good team behind you." As you work to achieve success off the playing field, don't overlook the importance of building the kind of team that will help you gain that success.

## Practice Time

In the business world, one kind of support team is called a "network." This team consists of all the people you know who might be able to help you find a job. Even when you're not job-hunting, it's important to maintain this vital network—because in today's business environment, you never know when you might need it!

- Compile a "networking" list of all the people you can think of who might be able to help you land the post-athletic job (or internship, or summer job) you are looking for.

- Set a goal to contact at least three of these people per week. If they can't offer you a job, ask them if they can give you the names of additional people to contact who might be able to offer you something.

# 23
# KEEPING ALL THE BALLS IN THE AIR
## Managing (and Making the Most of) Your Time

### The Game Plan

In this chapter, I will talk about:

- why good time managers are *self*-managers
- barriers that can keep you from managing your time well
- the "Three P's" of time management

*Gymnasts must learn to focus on what they are doing at the moment to do the job well, because the training is so time consuming. And I think one reason many gymnasts are also successful in other areas of their lives, particularly academics, is because they have acquired those time-management skills so early in life.*
- Katalin Deli, women's gymnastic coach, University of Minnesota

*I know for a fact companies are looking for people with a sports background because of the discipline skills and time management.*
- Judi Brown King, track and field coach and Olympic silver medalist

Time management skills are absolutely necessary for one to successfully manage athletic, academic, and social activities. At the collegiate level athletes spend at least as much time on sports as they do on academics. The only way to survive as an athlete and a student is to manage time well.

Milt Newton, a former championship college basketball player working toward a graduate degree in sports administration, said efficient time management was key to his academic success.

"As a freshman and sophomore, it was difficult," Newton told a *USA Today* reporter. "I said I didn't have time to study.

When you get older—junior and senior year—you see all the time you have to mess around. When you're traveling on a plane, you can read a textbook rather than sleep or read a comic book. The time you spend watching television, you could have been studying."

As you pursue success in the real world, time management becomes even more critical. That's why the time management industry does such a good business!

Still, though all those seminars and books on time management offer a variety of suggestions and techniques for managing time, they fail to acknowledge one very important truth: Deep down, you probably already know how to manage your time; you just aren't doing it.

If you think I'm wrong, just ask yourself this: Why are people seldom late for a flight, but they're often late for meetings, practices, or personal appointments? The answer is simple. People will wait, but planes won't—and we all take advantage of that fact.

## Time Management vs. Self-Management

Before we go any further, let's stop and take a closer look at the term "time management." When Milt Newton's study habits improved, was it due to his suddenly finding more time to study? No. The time had been there all along—it just took Milt a while to discover it.

What Milt really learned wasn't how to manage his time better; it was how to manage himself better. Time is static. It doesn't change. We all have 24 hours in a day. How we use that time is what changes.

To better manage yourself and make the most of your time, you first need to identify those things that may be causing poor self-management skills. Here are some of the more common problems:

• Lack of written personal goals with target dates
• Personal disorganization
• Overcommitment

- Procrastination
- Indecisiveness
- Fatigue
- Poor Planning
- Perfectionism
- Lack of self-discipline
- Ineffective calendar system
- Lack of motivation
- Interruptions
- Pessimism or negativity
- Unrealistic expectations
- Preoccupation with personal problems

If you look at this list closely, you'll probably find that most, if not all, of these items have at one time or another hampered your ability to use your time well. Take procrastination, for example. We've all put things off at one time or another for a variety of reasons. Sometimes we just have a hard time making up our minds, or we enjoy the adrenaline rush that comes from having to do things at the last minute. Sometimes we procrastinate because we're afraid of failing. This could be a problem for the athlete making the transition from an area where he or she is very successful to an area where success might not come as easily.

Procrastination isn't always bad. After all, we can't do everything at once (if we try, then that's poor time management). Some things have to be put off. It's *what* you put off that you need to look at. When you're putting off things that are important and that have deadlines or time frames, then you're procrastinating.

If procrastination is a habit that's affecting your self-management skills, here are some tips for overcoming it:

- *Look at how you procrastinate.*

Do you generally procrastinate at the beginning, middle, or end of a project? When you know how you delay, you can head yourself off at the pass. For instance, some people are what I call "Stop-and-Snackers." They can never start something without having to stop and go get something to eat or drink. If you're a "Stop-and-Snacker," get out your chips and dip before you start to work. Then you have no excuse to get up later.

• *Have a clear goal.*

The more specific you are, the more likely you are to get results. I recall hearing of one famous writer who set himself a goal of writing a certain number of words each day. Sometimes it might take him two hours, sometimes it would take 10 or 12. But he had a goal and he stuck to it.

• *Choose to do it.*

Whenever we say that we "have" to do something, it sounds negative. Few of us enjoy doing things we "have" to do. Instead, say "I choose to do this." This puts you in control.

• *Schedule your time.*

I have a friend who hates to make phone calls. She'll procrastinate making phone calls all day, until it's finally too late to get in touch with anyone. The only way she can bring herself to get on the phone is to schedule a time first thing in the morning to make her calls and get them out of the way.

• *Start small.*

Big tasks are overwhelming. So break big things into little pieces. Instead of saying, "I will write my term paper today," say, "I will assemble my research materials today."

## The Three P's of Time Management

As I mentioned earlier, you probably already know what you need to do to manage your time better. Just look at the appointments you aren't late for, or the projects you do finish on time. In these instances, chances are you have done three important things. These are the "Three P's" of time management: Prioritize, Plan, and Protect.

1) *Prioritize.*

When setting your priorities, there are two famous laws to remember. The first is "Parkinson's Law." It states that work tends to expand to fill the time allotted for its completion. "Parkinson's Law" makes setting priorities crucial because if you don't know what your priorities are, you might fill up all your time working on less important things.

The second law, "Pareto's Principle," states that 80 percent of your results come from 20 percent of your efforts. This is called the 80-20 rule. The implication is that you need to spend more time on the high priority activities that will bring you the greatest rewards.

Sometimes people have a hard time deciding what their priorities are. Everything seems important, so how do they choose? If this is your problem, ask yourself the following questions:

> (1) Of all the things I have to do, which ones will contribute the most toward achieving my goals?
>
> (2) What are the most immediate things to be done, and why should I do them first?
>
> (3) What are the things that get in the way of my achieving my goals, and why do they happen?

2) *Plan.*

Once you decide on your priorities, plan how you will carry them out. Using a daily and weekly "to do" list is a valuable aid. It's a good idea to make your "to do" list at the same time every day. This way you'll get into the habit of doing it. While you're at it, note how much time each item on your list should take to complete. This will help you avoid spending too much time on any one thing.

3) *Protect.*

When you've established your priorities and made your plans, you must then protect that time. This has a lot to do with saying "no" to internal and external distractions that will keep you from getting things done.

No matter what your time management skills are, it is how motivated you are to use them (in other words, how good you are at managing your*self*) that will make the difference.

My experience in the business and counseling fields has led me to believe that most people manage their lives by crisis. They are driven by external events. When you manage your time (and yourself), what you are doing is gaining control over your life. You are putting yourself in the driver's seat.

## Practice Time

There is never enough time to do everything. Make sure the important things get done by using the following technique:

1. Every night make a list of the things you need to do the next day.

2. Write "A" in front of the most important ones—the things that *have* to be done. Write "B" in front of the next important, "should do" things. Write "C" in front of the rest.

3. When you begin the day by working on your high priority tasks, you'll find that your energy and enthusiasm usually increases while your stress level decreases.

# 24
# READING THE OPPOSITION
## Sharpening Your Problem-Solving Skills

### The Game Plan

In this chapter, I will talk about:

- why we need problems in order to be happy
- some of the different ways we solve problems
- the five stages of problem solving

*Those things that hurt, instruct.*
- Benjamin Franklin

Nobody likes problems. Unfortunately, problems are life's normal state of affairs. Someone once said, "A man who has no problems is out of the game." In other words, dead. It's hard to get through a day without at least one problem cropping up, whether big (losing a job) or little (losing your car keys). What you may not realize is that problems—and how we solve them—are a key part of living a happy, successful life.

The ability to face and solve problems is critical to our self-esteem. Every time we confront a problem instead of running away from it, we feel a little bit better about ourselves. Facing our problems shows maturity and capability. Problem-solving enables us to learn and progress. When we're unable to solve problems, we've "hit the wall," so to speak. We're stopped progressing.

Problem-solving comes naturally to few people (otherwise, there would be fewer problems in this world!). As an athlete, however, you probably have unrealized problem-solving skills. Competition and problems go hand-in-hand. In competition, you always run into new challenges. Maybe the weather isn't in your favor. Maybe you're in a slump. Maybe your opponent is more skilled in certain areas than you are. Whatever the challenge is, you have to recognize it and overcome it. Just as the tennis player adjusts her grip to return the ball, and the defensive lineman moves in response to the shifting offense, you have to learn to make adjustments in your game. That is what problem-solving is all about.

The better competitor you are, the better your problem-solving abilities. What you need is to recognize those skills and learn how to apply them to the real world.

## More Than One Way to Skin a Cat

*Anyone who can spell a word only one way is an idiot.*
   - W.C. Fields

My years as a counselor and consultant (fancy names for a professional problem-solver) help me to appreciate W.C. Fields' point. Obstacles can usually be overcome in more than one way. Some problems, such as whether you were overcharged in a business transaction, demand facts and analysis. Other problems, such as what to do with a rebellious child, require a more intuitive approach. Some problems are solved through a process of discovery—the pieces just fall into place, while others fall into the trial-and-error category, where you keep trying until you finally stumble across the solution.

When trying to solve a problem, it helps to determine what method will be most effective. Being factual and analytical, for example, when a difficulty needs to be handled intuitively, can make the problem worse.

## The Five Stages of Problem-Solving

Most successful problem-solving involves five stages:

1) admitting or recognizing the problem
2) defining its dimensions
3) generating possible ways to solve it
4) evaluating those solutions for the best one
5) creating an action plan employing the best solution

• *Stage One: Admitting the Problem*

You can't solve a problem unless you first face it. Often, we fail to admit that a difficulty exists, or see the real problem, because *we* are part of it. An athlete who's not getting much playing time may place all the blame on the coach rather than looking inwardly to identify his or her own weaknesses. Likewise, the owner of a failing business may fault the economy without ever admitting that changes need to be made in the company.

• *Stage Two: Defining the Problem*

A problem well defined is a problem partly solved. Let's take the athlete who's sitting on the bench most of the time. When that athlete stops saying, "I'm sitting on the bench because the coach dislikes me," and starts saying, "I'm sitting on the bench because my skills are not as good as the rest of the players," then that gives the athlete a goal. Only when we are aware of the real problem can we work constructively to eliminate it.

• *Stage Three: Generating Solutions*

As the problem becomes clearer, options begin to emerge. Come up with as many options as possible and write them down. Recognize that there can be many ways to handle the problem. In basketball, if one defense isn't working, you try another. So don't cut off your imagination. Sometimes the last idea is the best one.

• *Stage Four: Evaluating Solutions*

At this point, we weed out good ideas from bad—or the better from the good! Evaluate each possible solution. Consider the resources necessary to carry out the planned remedy. Are these resources available? Are they appropriate? Estimate the probability of success for each alternative. Weed out the unfeasible and select the two or three most likely solutions. Then make your decision.

• *Stage Five: Creating an Action Plan*

Put your decision into action! Establish your game plan. Decide where you want to go and anticipate your obstacles. Decide what's needed to overcome these obstacles. Set time limits.

Weigh the strengths and weaknesses of your plan as you go and make appropriate adjustments.

If you can, experiment. Try out your chosen solution. If you're deciding on a college, pick one and go there in your mind for a day or two. How does your college of choice feel? If it doesn't feel right, maybe you'd better think it over again.

Whatever method you use for solving your problems, remember that a good life is not problem-free. Rather it is one in which problems are confronted with honesty, discipline, and the willingness to work them out.

## Practice Time

Think of a problem facing you at this time in your life. Maybe you're having difficulties with a teacher, coach, or parent. Perhaps you'd like to overcome a personal habit. Or maybe it involves a choice—what school to go to, whether you should get married, what kind of job to look for, and so on.

• Determine to solve your problem. First, think of what will happen if you do nothing about the problem. How will you feel? How will it affect your self-image? Now, visualize yourself successfully solving the problem. How do you feel? What kind of self-image do you have?

• Apply the five stages of problem-solving to your problem. As you go through the process, continually remind yourself of how you will feel when you successfully reach a solution.

# 25
# THE BIG SAVE
## Planning Your Financial Future

### The Game Plan

In this chapter, I will talk about:

- why financial planning is important for everyone, regardless of age or financial status
- how saving when you're young will enable you to spend when you're old
- financial planning tips

*Athletes have been told by others for their entire life-they won't make it. So they learn to put up a shield against such comments. Unfortunately, this shield also inhibits them from prudent financial planning because they believe there will always be one more contract.*

*- Paul McDonald, former NFL Player, current Merrill Lynch financial consultant-sports*

*I was in no danger of becoming one of those tragic, or sometimes only pathetic, former professional athletes whose money vanishes even faster than their fame once they retire. Since the start of my professional career in 1969, I had a financial manager, and I had made it my business to know my finances.*

*- Arthur Ashe, Days of Grace*

According to a report in *USA Today*, almost 30 percent of 2,000 high school students recently polled expected to earn between $30,000 and $40,000 upon finishing their education. That expectation is about as realistic as making the pros is for all those young athletes who count on that day coming.

Given the state of today's economy, individuals of all ages

must learn how to manage their finances and plan for their financial futures.

If you are a top athlete, you may think that all you have to do is work hard enough to be offered a professional contract, and then you'll have so much money you won't have to worry about finances. The truth is, few people ever have enough money that they don't have to worry about it. Even the Queen of Great Britain, one of the richest people in the world, worries about money. Athletic success doesn't guarantee financial success. There are all too many athletes who made millions and are bankrupt before the age of 40.

## Making (and Keeping!) Your Money

Planning for your financial future involves two things. First, you must determine how you're going to make your money (this is called career planning). Then you must plan how you're going to keep your money (this is called financial planning).

One of the main goals of financial planning is to manage your money well enough so that you can support yourself at retirement. Young people find it hard to think about retirement. Even we old people find it hard! But think about it you must.

You can't just assume that when you get old, you will be taken care of. Fewer companies offer pension plans these days, and fewer people stay with any one company long enough to collect one. Social security may not be there for you, either—at least, not enough to live on, comfortably. That's why, for most of us, planning for retirement means saving and investing our money wisely.

If you acquire the saving habit while you're young, it will be that much easier for you when you get older. However, that's easier said than done. Young people live in a world of immediate gratification (athletes even more so). For kids, a stereo in the hand is worth two CDs (the money kind—not the music kind) in the bank.

Kids aren't the only ones who could be better savers. Most people could save more than they do, but they lack the will power. Don't let this be *your* excuse for not saving. I believe that if you have the will power necessary to be successful at your sport, you can find the will necessary to save money.

The payoff for starting young is big. For example, if you start at age 25 to invest $2,000 a year, by the time you turn 65, you could have earned close to $600,000. However, if you wait until you're 35 to start saving, your nest egg will be less than half that much. That $20,000 you didn't save between the ages of 25 and 35 could end up costing you over $300,000!

## Financial Planning Tips

In his memoirs, Arthur Ashe offered some financial counsel to the "instant millionaires" we see being created in the sports world today. The counsel would hold true for just about anyone, however.

First, he urged them to have a financial plan. When you set financial goals and priorities, it's less easy to be sidetracked by unnecessary things.

Next, he advised them to seek out the best people they could find to help them with their legal and financial matters. He also cautioned them to read everything before they signed it, and then to stick to the agreements they made. He concluded by saying that these young stars needed to be careful about being too generous. While charity is important, one's own financial obligations should come first.

## Planning For Your Financial Future

I would like to add my own set of financial planning tips to those of Ashe's:

• *Choose a major carefully.*
Don't choose a major because it's easy or because it will allow you more time to concentrate on sports or because all your friends are choosing it. Arthur Ashe's degree was in business administration. That certainly helped him understand the importance of managing his finances well.

While deciding on a major, you naturally need to take into

consideration the things you like to do and that you're good at doing. But you should also think in terms of "What kind(s) of job(s) will a degree in this subject help me to get?" Investigate the job market. What jobs are likely to be most in demand in the future? [*United States Department of Occupational Outlook Handbook 1988.* Washington, D.C., U.S. Government Printing Office.] What jobs will pay you what you hope to earn?

• *Get your degree.*
   Even if you make the pros, you're more likely to end up a journeyman athlete rather than the next Michael Jordan. Chances are, one day you'll need something else to fall back on. Don't make the mistake of thinking that a fat contract will protect you from ever having money problems, or from having to eventually go out and get a "real job."

**My generation was probably the last in which young athletes made large amounts of money and were also college graduates. Just as the open era transformed my sport, so did free agency transform the other sports and reduce the incentive for a superior athlete to finish college, or even to take it seriously... Often, even with rich contracts, these athletes are on their way to being paupers. Not only are they naive in handling legal and financial matters; they often lack the one quality that might save them: The ability to interact in a prudent, respectful way with their lawyers and financial managers. Many young athletes are probably doomed, tragically, to return to the poverty from which sport almost saved them."**
   **- Arthur Ashe, *Days of Grace***

• *Learn the basics of financial management.*
   Everyone should know how to balance a checkbook (or at least keep it in good enough shape that you're not always bouncing checks). You should also learn how to budget. How to pay bills. How to invest. With interest rates being what they are these days, just putting your money in a savings account isn't enough. You need to learn about things like stocks, bonds, and

mutual funds. It may all seem like another language to you, but don't let yourself be intimidated.

Don't think you can get out of this by handing all your money over to a financial planner, either. The purpose of any financial planner shouldn't be to manage your money for you, it should be to teach *you* how to manage your money.

• *Avoid debt.*

Some debt is pretty much unavoidable. Few of us can afford to pay cash for a new car or house. Other debt *is* avoidable, and should be avoided like the plague. If you really want to buy something, do like one young couple I know: Instead of buying the item on credit, make "payments" to yourself. Put a set amount of money in an envelope each month until you've saved enough to pay for what you need.

• *Be disciplined.*

Again, your sports training can come through for you here. You know about discipline. Use it! When you go shopping, use the "wait and want" principle. If you see something you want, wait. If you still want it a week later, go back for it.

A lot of people think financial planning is something for rich people, or for "business-minded" people, or for just about anyone but themselves. The truth is, anyone can—and should—become a financial planner. And the sooner you start, the better.

## Practice Time

There are so many practical things you can do to improve your financial future that it's hard to pick just a few. Here are some of my suggestions. See if you can come up with some exercises of your own, as well.

- Set a financial goal (i.e.; saving enough for a down-payment on a car, paying off a credit card debt, buying the latest model of athletic shoes). Using the goal-setting techniques you learned earlier, map out a plan for achieving your financial goal.

- Pick an area of financial management that you are weak in (for example, balancing a checkbook). Find an "expert" who can teach you how to be better at this subject.

- Learn more about the investment world. Banks, brokerage houses, accounting firms, and other members of the financial industry often offer free seminars, retirement planning kits, magazines, and software programs.

- Play the stock market (on paper) by pretending you have $1,000 to invest. What stocks would you buy? Why? Follow the progress of your stocks for one month. Did you earn or lose money?

# 26
# LETTING OFF STEAM
## Making Stress Work For (Not Against) You

### The Game Plan

In this chapter, I will talk about:

- what stress is, how it affects you, and how to manage it
- factors that can lead athletes to depression and suicide
- symptoms of depression
- strategies for avoiding depression

*Stress is here to stay. You need to learn to live with it.*
- David Reynolds, Ph.D. and stress-control instructor

As an athlete, you are no stranger to stress. There is the stress of competition. There is the stress of trying to make the team. There are the pressures that come with attempting to balance sports with school, family, or a host of other obligations.

Some athletes become very good at handling this stress. Others find it harder to cope. Still others are surprised to discover that, although they deal very well with the stresses of the sports world, they have difficulty in handling the stresses of the real world.

For better or worse, stress is a part of life. We usually think of stress as something bad. That's not necessarily true, however. A little bit of stress helps you concentrate, focus, and meet challenges. It's too much stress that impedes your performance. That's why it's important to recognize what stress is, how it affects you, and how you can successfully manage it.

### Defining Stress

Stress is your physical and emotional reaction to change. It can result from positive changes (marriage or the birth of a baby) or from negative ones (the death of a loved one or loss of a job). Harmful stress usually results from numerous or drastic changes in life.

Positive reactions to stress include zest for living, enthusiasm for getting things done, and increased productivity. When under excessive stress, however, you are more likely to experience the following: persistent anxiety, fatigue, insomnia, poor concentration, irritability, dizzy spells, indecisiveness, depression, persistent remorse, or thoughts of dying. Excessive stress increases your susceptibility to a wide range of physical conditions such as colds, flu, high blood pressure, and other illnesses.

You can learn how to respond positively to stress, but you have to really want to do so. I've known people who seem to derive a lot of enjoyment from complaining about how stressful their lives are. On the other hand, I've known people who have experienced terrible catastrophes in their lives, and yet you would never know it by their actions or attitudes.

## Controlling Stress

### Laughter is inner jogging.
- Norman Cousins

Many things keep stress from getting out of control. The main goal of these stress-busters isn't to help you get rid of stress (because there's no such thing as a completely stress-free life); it's to help you learn how to live with the stress you do have.

### Stress Busters

1) *Recognize your peak stress times.*
Throughout the day, there are certain brain chemicals that rise and fall, making you more prone to feeling stressed. For example, early morning is generally a high-stress time. Try to schedule things so that you don't have a lot of stressful stuff going on during the times when you're less able to handle it. In addition, learn to recognize stress "warning signs." These would include any changes in behavior that might be the result of stress.

2) *Prevent crashes.*

Our bodies have certain rhythms of productive time and down time. Learn to recognize when you need to take down time. For example, if you've had a burst of productive work or great thinking, and then feel the need to stretch or move around, that's a down-time signal. When we ignore those signals, we wear ourselves out and that makes us more susceptible to stress. So listen to your body. Take a break.

3) *Control yourself.*

Too many people use stress as an excuse for out-of-control behavior. If you want to reduce stress, kicking the dog won't do it. You have to feel in control, which means controlling your reactions. You need to accept your feelings, but don't focus on them. That means saying to yourself, "I'm feeling stressed right now. What can I do to improve the situation?"

4) *Avoid too many big changes.*

Some changes are unavoidable. Whenever possible, however, try to keep from having to handle too many changes at once. For example, one mistake many people make is to immediately sell their house after losing a spouse to death or divorce. This only makes a stressful situation more stressful. A better plan would be to remain in the home for at least six months, and then consider selling it.

5) *Be healthy.*

The healthier you are, the more energy you'll have to handle stress. There are three main components to good health:

• Sleep. Without enough of it, you can't think clearly and are in poor shape to handle problems that come up.

• Exercise. Like Charles Barkley has said, "Exercise is important, because if you don't take care of your body, it won't take care of you." Be careful not to exercise too much, though, or you could end up too tired to successfully manage stress.

• Diet. What you eat (and when you eat it) can either help or hinder your ability to handle stress. Sugary foods, for example, give an energy boost that quickly wears off and leaves you feeling lower than before. You should also avoid non-prescription medications, drugs, or alcohol to relieve symptoms of stress. Drugs only provide temporary relief from tension. They can't cure the underlying cause.

## Depression: When Stress Becomes Too Much

*When I first had my operation, I got a lot of attention and that was a real source of encouragement; but, it also distracted me from digging down and realizing what had happened. Then one day, I woke up, looked in the mirror and didn't like what I saw. My arm, my livelihood, was gone. That's when I went into depression.*
- Dave Dravecky, *USA Today*, February 10, 1992

Sometimes, despite our best intentions, stress overwhelms us and depression sets in. Depression is the country's No.1 mental disorder. An estimated 10 percent of Americans suffer from depression at any one time, and at least 10 percent will experience a period of major depression sometime during their lives.

Depression isn't limited to adults. According to the American Association of Pediatrics and the American Medical Association, mental disorders affect 634,000 adolescents nationwide. Over the past 20 years, the suicide rate tripled among 10- to 14-year-olds and doubled among 15- to 19-year-olds.

## Athletes and Depression

Athletes are not immune to depression, either, even though many people think they are. Over and over, with athletes who commit suicide, the refrain you hear is, "He was such a competitor. Such a fighter. I can't believe he gave up like this." The thought seems to be, "How could someone with so much talent have anything to be depressed about?"

There are many factors that can lead athletes to depression, and even suicide. Ken Griffey, Jr., of the Seattle Mariners, revealed that as a young baseball player the pressure he felt led to a depression that only ended after he tried to kill himself by overdosing on aspirin.

"What I've noted," said Loren Coleman, a researcher who has made a study of suicides among baseball players, "is that there seems to be an extended adolescence with ballplayers, and when they leave baseball they too often don't have coping mechanisms, or a solid support system from the ball clubs. They're just left to drift by themselves."

When the moment comes when you have to step away from all that sports have given you—identity, belonging, adulation, purpose—depression is likely to occur. Bruce Gardner fashioned the best pitching record (40-5) in the University of Southern California's history. And yet, on the night of June 5, 1971, just a short distance from the field where he had experienced his finest moments, Bruce Gardner killed himself. Paul Fegen, Gardner's cousin, was quoted as saying, "Brucie had everything going for him. I mean *everything*. But he couldn't succeed as readily in life as he did with his athletic ability and charm."

Much of the time, the suffering that results from depression goes unrecognized and untreated. People (men, especially) tend to not take depression very seriously, even though those who have experienced both a major physical illness and depression usually say that the depression was much harder to handle.

Sometimes an athlete's focus on strength and self-reliance prevents him or her from seeking help just when it's needed most. One NBA player who attempted suicide after suffering from clinical depression said, "Trying to appear as if everything is all right is detrimental...I think I need to get everything into the open to get well."

Dave Dravecky was lucky—he had a wife who knew how important it was to seek counseling. It was through that counseling that Dravecky was able to admit his fears and depression over losing his arm and find a way to overcome those fears.

## Symptoms of Depression

Before you can fight depression, you have to recognize it. That can be difficult.

Depression is more than just feeling sad or blue. How can you tell if you are seriously depressed? Here are some symptoms to look for:

• *Mood*

When you're depressed, you feel depressed. For many people, this feeling manifests itself as a loss of interest in or enjoyment of various activities such as going out with friends, eating, exercising, or having sex.

• *Mind*

When you're depressed, your mind doesn't work the way it should. You find it harder to concentrate, remember things, and make decisions. You experience a vague anxiety. You just know something awful is about to happen, but you don't know what it is. You become very negative about yourself and about life.

• *Body*

Your appetite usually changes and a sudden weight loss or gain is not unusual. Sleeping is more difficult. You don't have your usual energy. You may have such gastrointestinal symptoms as nausea or constipation.

• *Behavior*

Common behavior symptoms include tearfulness, a stooped posture, pacing, and restlessness. Some people may turn to drinking, drugs, extramarital affairs, or divorce. This kind of behavior is known as "acting out." The most serious form of acting out is suicide.

Even with the above guidelines, depression can still be difficult to diagnose. The boundary between normal, temporary feelings of sadness or discouragement, and real depression is not sharply defined.

## Chasing Away the Blues

What if the depression isn't serious? What if it's a milder case—the kind that people refer to when they sigh and say, "I'm depressed"—when what they really mean is that they're feeling gloomy or disheartened? In this case, try these strategies to keep true depression at bay:

1) *Make friends with your depression.*

Treat it like an old acquaintance who has dropped by to tell you something you need to hear. Depression is your body's way of telling you that something is wrong. Invite it to stay just long enough to tell you why it has come and what it's message is.

2) *Talk to someone.*

Talk to someone you trust. Gather information, get objective feedback, and allow others to express their sympathy and concern.

3) *Look at the Big Picture.*

Debi Thomas was devastated when she failed to win the gold medal in the 1988 Winter Olympics. But then she saw that things weren't so bad after all. "I realized that life isn't over," Thomas said. "Before the Olympics, I thought if you don't win, you're going to die. Thank goodness I made a lot of good decisions early on with school. I have a chance to get a degree at Stanford and more than a few successful people have come out of Stanford. It didn't matter that I didn't win…what happened, happened. Now I'm going to get on with my life."

4) *Think rationally.*

When you're depressed, it can be hard to know whether or not you're thinking rationally. Ask yourself the following:

• Are my thoughts based on facts?
• Are they helping me protect myself?
• Will they help me get what I want?
• Are they helping me feel the way I want to feel?
• Are they helping me prevent unwanted conflict with others?

5) *Relax.*

It is important to take time for yourself and not to feel guilty about it. Relaxation time is important for two reasons: it gives you time to rest, and it gives you time to think. Sometimes people who are depressed fill up every moment of their day with activities to keep them from thinking about their problems. Their hope is that if they don't think about them, they'll go away. But that doesn't happen. The only way to get rid of a problem is to confront it and solve it.

6) *Learn from your depression.*

A friend of mine went through a period of depression in college when her boyfriend of three years broke off their relationship. It was not a pleasant experience, but it taught her something. Several years later when another serious relationship came to an end, she knew that she would survive because she had done so before.

Wendy Williams, a championship diver who has had several periods of depression in her life, expressed it this way: "Oh, what a learning experience. It's sort of a broader sense of knowledge that's stored away for the rest of my life and will help me get through other hard times."

## Riding the Rollercoaster

One way to think of depression is to compare it to a muscle cramp. Ignore it and it just gets worse. You've got to work it out. The most important thing to remember when coping with depression or any of life's stressful situations is that *you're* in the driver's seat. No matter what happens around you, you are still in control of *you*.

We're all going to have our ups and downs. Life is like a rollercoaster in that respect. You'll be chugging along without a care when, all of a sudden, the bottom drops out from under you. You can't get off, so you might as well enjoy the ride as a whole, even if some parts are less pleasant than others.

## Practice Time

### *Working It Out #1*

Relaxing is a good way to beat stress. Relaxing doesn't come naturally for a lot of folks—it has to be learned. Try the following relaxation technique whenever you're feeling stressed:

• Sit quietly in a comfortable position with your eyes closed.

• Relax all muscles, beginning with your feet and progressing upward. Keep them relaxed.

• Breathe through your nose and be aware of your breathing. For example, each time you breathe out, say a one syllable word, such as "one," silently. Breathe naturally and easily.

• Continue for 10-20 minutes, but don't use an alarm to time yourself. Follow this by sitting quietly for several minutes, first with your eyes closed, then opened. Continue to sit for a few minutes.

• Maintain a passive attitude, permitting relaxation to happen as it will. If you have distracting thoughts, try to ignore them by repeating the one-syllable word again. Do not dwell on distracting thoughts. Practice this technique once or twice a day.

### *Working It Out #2*

Are you depressed? Learn to recognize the symptoms of depression. The following inventory can help you:

#### Are You Depressed?

Review your life over the last six months. Then read each of the following items and rate how often the symptom is true of you.

**(1) Rarely   (2) Sometimes True   (3) Often True
(4) Frequently True   (5) Usually True**

_____ 1. I feel tired even when I've gotten adequate sleep.

_____ 2. I often feel discouraged.

_____ 3. I feel sad for no apparent reason.
_____ 4. I am forgetful.
_____ 5. I am irritable and sometimes snap at people.
_____ 6. I am withdrawn.
_____ 7. I have trouble sleeping.
_____ 8. I get sick a lot.
_____ 9. My attitude about school and/or work is "why bother."
_____ 10. I am not getting along with others.
_____ 11. My performance at school and/or work has slipped.
_____ 12. I use alcohol and/or drugs to feel better.
_____ 13. My relationships are strained.
_____ 14. I am having difficulty concentrating.
_____ 15. I am easily bored.
_____ 16. I feel frustrated.
_____ 17. I feel guilty.
_____ 18. I don't like what I'm doing with my life.
_____ 19. Social activities are draining.
_____ 20. Sex is not worth the effort.

Scoring:
20 - 40    You're doing well.
41 - 60    You're okay if you take preventative action.
61 - 80    You're a candidate for depression.
81 - 100   You're probably depressed.

Symptoms vary from person to person, but people with clinical depression will have at least some or perhaps all, of the above symptoms. Your doctor can determine whether or not your symptoms are caused by clinical depression.

# 27
# CLEARING THE HURDLE
## Overcoming Addictions That
## Can Hurt Your Game

### The Game Plan

In this chapter, I will talk about:

• why athletes are not immune to substance abuse
• what addiction is and how you can recognize it
• how you can work on overcoming addictions

*Some people get involved with drugs in order to be closer to the oppo-site sex ... some to be part of a group. Then there were some that were so curious, they wanted to know. I was a mixture of all of them. I knew that drugs were dangerous, but I never expected that I would get hooked, which is probably the dumbest excuse, but it's the truth. Everybody thinks that they can control [drugs]. But they can't; drugs control you.*
- Lonnie Smith, Atlanta Braves, *San Diego Union*, April 21, 1989

*How can I explain addiction? Alcoholics, overeaters, we're never satisfied with who or where we are. When the world was telling me "You're great," I'd say to myself, "What the hell's so great about me? I don't even like me."*
- Baseball pitcher Steve Howe, *People*, July 29, 1991

It's ironic that a profession that emphasizes physical well-being could ever have a problem with substance abuse. And yet we hear stories every day of athletes who are suspended for drug use or arrested for drunk driving. Why does this happen?

There are many reasons. The pressure to succeed, the need to recapture the "highs" of competition, the down time on road trips when boredom and loneliness set in (without other interests to alleviate the emotional void), the lack of tools to handle emotions and feelings (other than boredom and loneliness)—these all can lead an athlete to drug or alcohol abuse.

There are other contributors, as well. A successful athlete must have confidence in his or her ability to perform. This confidence, however, can lead to what is called the "Superman" syndrome, where athletes believe they are immune to the addictions that afflict lesser mortals. It's the adolescent mentality in action. Young and gifted athletes often think that they can handle anything. Perhaps that is one reason Jennifer Capriati, a tennis sensation at age 14, found herself under arrest for possession of marijuana at age 18.

When it comes to athletes and drug use, one needs to look at the kind of drug and why it's being used. In the sports world, drugs fall into three different categories:

## Painkillers

Eric Show, a winning pitcher for the San Diego Padres, died at age 37 at a private drug treatment center. Show had overdosed on heroin and cocaine. A former teammate of Show's linked his drug problems to a 1989 back injury and the drugs Show had to take in order to play.

All athletes experience times when they must play hurt. The use of painkillers, therefore, is widespread. Still, just because a painkiller is given by a team doctor doesn't make it harmless. These drugs are as potentially addictive as any other.

## Performance-Enhancers

The farther you go in the sports world, the higher the stakes. The athlete who got by on natural ability in high school often finds that he or she's just an average player in college. And so they take something (like steroids) to give them an edge. Steroids do improve athletic performance. They also cause a wide range of side effects, including stunted growth, aggressiveness, depression, paranoia, high blood pressure, and impotence. Despite this overwhelming medical evidence, many athletes view steroid use as a necessary part of becoming a serious competitor.

## Recreational Drugs

Do sports encourage individuals to use such recreational drugs as alcohol and tobacco? That's a controversial question. There's no doubt that alcohol, especially beer, is associated with the sports world. For the top-level athlete, alcohol is a depressant that can be used to relax from the extreme pressure of the game. Baseball players say the same thing about chewing tobacco—it helps them relax. The costs, however, can be great. Just ask Rick Bender, a Californian in his 30s who lost most of the lower half of his face to cancer and infections resulting from chewing tobacco. Bender said he started chewing when he was 12 because he was an avid baseball player, all the big-league players chewed, and "it was billed as a safe alternative to smoking."

## Defining Addiction

Rick Bender probably never thought of himself as an addict. After all, chewing tobacco was supposed to be "safe." However, it's possible to become addicted to just about anything, safe or not.

Anything that has more power over you than you do is an addiction. You are addicted when your use of something becomes abuse—excessive with negative medical or social consequences. A person can be addicted to food, sex, exercise, work, or religion. Almost anything good can be made bad by lack of moderation.

Take gambling, for example. Lots of people enjoy buying their weekly lottery ticket or spending a few dollars' worth of nickels on their way through Vegas. If it never goes any further than that, there's no problem. It's when you fall into the Pete Rose Syndrome that trouble arises. After Rose was barred from baseball because of his gambling, he said, "I know I can't gamble on anything anymore, because I can't control it." Just a few short years later, Rose was quoted as saying, "I'm not going to sit here and tell you I don't gamble. What's the big deal?" The big deal is this: underestimating the power of an addiction can ruin you.

Still, this "big deal" traps many athletes. When Olympic speed skater Mary Doctor initially decided to seek treatment for her drug and alcohol problem, she chose less intensive outpatient therapy instead of the recommended residential treatment program. After four months of sobriety, Doctor backslid at the 1991 world team trials in Wisconsin. She skated her races while stoned on marijuana. Eventually, Doctor wised up. She stopped underestimating her addiction and got the treatment she needed.

## Understanding Addiction

*What I had was not a drug problem but a living problem, I lived for all the wrong reasons.*
- John Lucas, coach of the Philadelphia 76ers

Addiction involves two problems: the addiction itself and the underlying problem masked or denied by the addiction. Such problems include poor self-esteem, depression, a troubled relationship, anxiety, or a biochemical abnormality (such as an allergy that may cause a person to have a different response to alcohol or other drugs).

Drug and alcohol abuse are the most common and destructive addictions among athletes. For athletes, these substances provide escape when the real world presses too close. Steve Howe once commented that: "Baseball's not a realistic world. It's something where I can escape." However, Howe couldn't spend 24 hours a day on the pitcher's mound. So he turned to drugs.

There are three characteristics of dependency or addiction: compulsion, loss of control, and negative consequences.

## Compulsion

"I was like an addict," say Hall-of-Famer Rod Carew, who substituted chewing tobacco for the 15-20 cans of Coke he drank during a game. "It was the first thing I'd do in the morning, before brushing my teeth, and the last thing before going to sleep."

Compulsion means you have a powerful emotional and/or physical dependency on the drug. You organize your life around it. For example:

• You only go to parties if alcohol will be there.
• You travel with a pocket flask or a stash of the drug.
• You begin to believe the drug is the only thing that can be counted on and trusted.

## Loss of Control

Once you begin using, how much you'll use or what will happen is unpredictable. You won't be able to reduce your use or abstain. For example:

• Use becomes like a game of Russian roulette—sometimes thrilling, always dangerous.
• You go out planning to have a few drinks with friends, wake up the next day hung over and sick—and looking forward to going out again that night.
• You plan to smoke only three cigarettes a day and are unable to do so.

## Negative Consequences

Drug abuse can have a negative effect on your self-esteem, competence, efficiency, health, personal relationships, work, finances, and relationship with the law. For example:

• Rod Carew accrued over $100,000 in dental bills during his 19-year career due to his habit of chewing tobacco.
• All-pro linebacker Lawrence Taylor was suspended and lost $250,000 when he tested positive for drug use.
• Darryl Strawberry, one of baseball's most talented (and troubled) players, was released from his contract with the San Francisco Giants after violating Major League Baseball's substance abuse policy for a second time.
• Mercury Morris, former star running back for the Miami

Dolphins, spent more than three years in prison after being convicted of selling cocaine. The conviction was later overturned, but Morris admitted he'd been so strung out on cocaine that he couldn't think straight.

• National Hockey League player John Kordic died of lung failure related to a malfunctioning heart, after it took eight police officers to subdue him in a Quebec City motel room where syringes and steroids were found.

## Overcoming Addiction

A lot of people think that getting clean is the hardest part of overcoming drug abuse, but it's not. Staying clean is. When Chip Banks, linebacker for the Indianapolis Colts, tested positive for cocaine use, he was threatened with being banned from football for life if he tested positive again. You'd think that would be a powerful motivation for staying away from drugs. Banks, aware that more than half the cocaine users who make it through therapy end up backsliding, knew it would be the toughest game of his life. As he said, "It's possible to stay clean ... It's also possible for me to mess up next week. You flip a coin every day."

Overcoming an addiction means acknowledging that you have a problem, accepting responsibility and working on a solution. John Lucas, for example, transferred his negative addiction to a positive one: helping other addicts overcome their problems. Lucas founded John Lucas Enterprises, which offers a variety of treatment, aftercare and outpatient programs for athletes and others.

Unfortunately, not all people with a substance abuse problem react as positively as John Lucas. Instead, they typically react in one of two ways. They may deny or minimize the extent of the problem (as seems to be the case with the majority of the nation's estimated 250,000 adolescent users of anabolic steroids), or they may admit there is a problem but blame others for it.

Spencer Haywood could testify to the latter. Haywood, a former forward with the Los Angeles Lakers, was kicked off the team in the middle of the 1980 championship series. At fault was Haywood's decreased playing ability due to drug use.

That's not how Haywood then saw it, however. As he said, "I was blaming everybody. Magic Johnson was putting too much spin on the passes. I needed some stickum to hold them. The coach didn't know how to use me. It was everybody else's fault. Paranoia had a field day with me."

Why is it so hard to admit to having a problem? Probably because it makes us feel ashamed, guilty, stupid, embarrassed, or afraid—feelings we prefer to avoid. Sometimes, though, we do just the opposite. Not only do we admit we have a problem, but we start feeling so guilty about it that the guilt and blame become almost as destructive as the addictive behavior.

Often people make the mistake of trying to treat the addiction without treating the problems that led to it. That's when you see people going back to the rehab center over and over again. John Lucas went through several treatment programs and relapsed every time. Finally, he confronted the problems that had him escaping from his own house to go on a drug and alcohol binge.

I think the key element in overcoming any addiction is understanding yourself. John Lucas would agree. "Sure, I had trophies and titles," he said. "I knew what they meant, but I didn't know who I was… Recovery has helped me find out who I am. What I thought was the worst curse has turned out to be the greatest blessing. I'm the best 'me' I've ever been."

## Practice Time

### What's Your Score?

The following questions will help you evaluate the role alcohol and other substances play in your life:

1. Do you lie or otherwise conceal how much you use?

2. Do you have blackouts or forget things that happened while you were using drugs or alcohol?

3. Do you ever miss work or school because you are under the influence of or recovering from using drugs or alcohol?

4. Have you ever decided to stop using the substance, but started using it again just a few days later?

5. Do you always use drugs or alcohol to deal with a certain situation (such as when you are depressed, when you are feeling insecure, or when you are celebrating)?

6. Do you drink or use drugs before you go to parties or bars to "prime" for the event?

7. Do you spend money on drugs or alcohol when you really need or want it for something else?

8. Have your family or friends ever told you that you drink or use drugs too much?

9. Do you do things under the influence that you regret when you are sober?

10. Do you drink or use drugs by yourself?

If you answered yes to any of these questions, you may want to take a look at the role alcohol or drugs plays in your life. If you answered yes to four or more, you should seek help in changing your lifestyle.

# 28
# GOING ONE-ON-ONE
## Improving Your Personal and Interpersonal Relationships

### The Game Plan

In this chapter, I will talk about:

- why relationship skills are so important to your personal and professional success
- what sports can teach you about relationships
- relationship barriers caused by sports
- the principles of building a good relationship

He:     *Then what is it your friends talk about out there?*

She:    *Well, real life...relationships...Are they working? Are they*
        *not? Who is she seeing, is that working?*

He:     *No contest. We win.*

She:    *Why?*

He:     *Honey, if that were as interesting as baseball, they'd have cards*
        *for it with gum.*
        - from the movie, *City Slickers*

*...The bond grew and grew, regardless of what our fortunes were on the*
*court and that was nice. That was part of the reason I decided to stay in*
*as long as I did. My being out there made Earvin's job a lot easier.*
*Earvin's being out there made my job easier. Look where we took it—all*
*the way to the top, and we kept it up there.*
        - Kareem Abdul-Jabbar, speaking of his relationship with Earvin "Magic"
        Johnson (*Los Angeles Times*, November 2, 1990)

Good relationships are essential to success. In her book, *The Androgynous Manager*, Alice Sargent reported that 85 percent of employees dismissed from their jobs were fired because they could not get along well with their coworkers. Only 12 percent were fired for incompetence.

To build good relationships, you need to develop your relationship, or interpersonal skills. Interpersonal skills are to real world success what physical skills are to athletic success. You simply can't do without them if you intend to have meaningful personal and professional relationships.

My own understanding of the importance of interpersonal skills increased when I began working as a consultant to business executives. At first I was apprehensive about how I could counsel these people on how to improve their businesses. After all, I was a psychologist, not a business expert. But after working closely with a number of chief executives, it became clear that 90 percent of the problems limiting the effectiveness of their companies weren't business problems—they were people problems. These companies needed to work at improving relationships before they could improve profits.

## Athletes and Relationships

When I first asked myself what sports can teach athletes about relationships, my initial thought was, "Not much." What a sad commentary. Giving it more thought, though, I came up with some sports-inspired ideas relevant to relationships:

• You have to give to receive. In sports you "give" endless hours of practice—you give that extra effort—to "receive" the payoff.

• It ain't over till it's over. People quit on relationships much too quickly. In my years of clinical practice, I observed that few people began therapy to save the relationship. Rather, most of them came to find reasons to leave the relationship. Sports teach you the principle of not giving up so easily.

• Forgive and forget. It doesn't do any good for an athlete to dwell on mistakes they or their teammates make. If someone screws up, you forgive them and move on. It's the only way to get back into the game.

In *Days of Grace*, Arthur Ashe spoke to his daughter, Camera, about the importance of forgiveness:

> Nowadays, people break up marriages over the slightest of differences, which is a pity. On the night before your mother and I were married, Jean Young, the wife of Andrew Young, the minister at our wedding, gave us some good advice. The most important ingredient in a marriage, she said, was forgiveness: the willingness of each partner to forgive the other. Forgiving takes courage, but it is the key…No marriage or truly important human relationship can survive, let alone flourish, without both partners willing to forgive.

• Gut checks are important. When athletes lose a contest, they are often encouraged to take a good look inside to see what it is they need to work on to win. The same applies to a relationship.

• You need to get excited. You have to be enthusiastic about your team, your game, whatever. That excitement is what propels you forward. If you aren't into a relationship, if you aren't excited about being with the other person, then the relationship probably won't last.

• Proximity doesn't equal closeness. Some people argue that the teamwork element of sports helps athletes build relationships. To a certain extent, that's true. Teamwork is people coming together, blending talent to obtain a common goal. This principle is the same whether you're part of an athletic team, a business team, or a family team. However, the camaraderie that is felt among members of an athletic team often goes no further than the locker room. I played with some really great guys during my basketball career. But at that time, to my discredit, I never saw them as anything other than fellow basketball players.

• Communication, fun, and friendship are among the keys to a successful relationship. Sports facilitate all three of these elements. "When we have prospective clients, we try to entertain them on the golf course," said the commerce director of one southwestern state. "There's no better way to learn about people and foster relationships than knocking the little white ball around."

Folk singer Joan Baez once said, "The easiest kind of relationship for me is with 10 thousand people. The hardest is with one." Athletes, perhaps, can relate to this. It can be easy to make a stadium full of anonymous fans love you, but hard to do the same with an individual who's close enough to see you as you really are.

Just what are some of the qualities athletics foster that don't necessarily work in relationships? First, there is intensity. Intensity is a positive attribute on the playing field, but it seldom contributes to a relationship. People like to move at their own pace. Pressuring them or coming on too strong or too fast will not change this.

Secondly, there is passivity. Many athletes fall into the trap of letting others make their decisions and do things for them. The coach calls the plays and the equipment manager cleans up the locker room mess. This doesn't work well in a relationship. The athlete must do his or her part to make good things happen in a relationship and in ensuring that the inevitable and necessary changes to strengthen a relationship take place.

Jealousy is the third quality that the sports experience often fosters in relationships. Trained to be competitive, the athlete is in danger of viewing relationships from a competitive perspective. Instead of focusing on what you're giving to a relationship, you get hung up on what you're getting from it. Worst yet, you keep score—and you're not happy if a friend or spouse appears to have more points.

Handling the expectations of others can be a fourth aspect of sports that may undermine your relationships. As an athlete, you may be placed on a pedestal. People may view you as a role model. Or they may think that because you're so good at one thing (sports), you'll be good at other things as well. Then, when you don't live up to their expectations, their anger and disappointment may be very difficult to handle.

Finally, problems can and often occur in relationships when the relationship focuses too much on the athlete. For example, if one child is heavily involved in youth sports, the other siblings may resent the time spent by parents taking the athlete to practice, attending games, and so on. A girlfriend, boyfriend, or spouse may be resentful of all the attention given to the athlete, while they're left in the background.

Another relationship problem found among athletes (and among men in general) is called the "adolescent response." One particular counseling session stands out as an example of such a response. My patient, a middle-aged man, said his wife had called him one morning to make sure he had directions to the restaurant where they'd be celebrating her daughter's high school graduation. As his wife was about to hang up, the man said, "Hey, I'm really, really busy at work today. Why don't you call me around 6:30 and remind me (about the dinner)." His wife somewhat coolly responded, "Look, if you're there, you're there. If you're not, you're not."

In talking about the incident with this man, I pointed out that his request signaled to his wife that his work was more important than building a family relationship. That was why she responded in a sharp manner. His reaction was, "Gee, I guess I really screwed up. I really messed that one up." He said that three or four times. I could tell, though, that he wasn't really getting it. His response was more like that of a child who makes a mistake, says he's sorry, and then goes right out and does the same thing all over again. What my client didn't understand was that sorry doesn't mean anything, unless you take the responsibility of trying to correct your error.

## Principles of a Good Relationship

*I have invested in friendship all my life.*
- Arthur Ashe

No one is immune from relationship problems. I have counseled hundreds of couples on how to improve their relationships, and, yet, several years ago my own marriage was in serious trouble. Physically and emotionally, my wife and I had drifted apart.

Finally, I decided to quit worrying about what I thought my wife should be doing to get our relationship back on track. Instead, I concentrated on applying everything I'd been teaching people for the last 30 years. In other words, I invested in our marriage, and the investment paid off.

The following principles proved useful in getting my marriage moving in the right direction. Most of them would apply to any kind of relationship that needs help.

• *Take care of your own side of the street.*

It doesn't do any good for me to stand on my side of the street and point out all the things you need to do to fix up your property when my own property is also in need of repair. I must first work on my own house and hope that you'll like what you see and want to bring your property up to the same level. It doesn't work in athletics or in real life to point out the other person's weaknesses or mistakes without first taking stock of your own.

• *Remember that love is something you do.*

In sports, there are always those athletes who talk a good game and those who play a good game—who let their performance speak for them. This is true in other aspects of life. It's what you do, not what you say. William Wordsworth said that the best part of a man's life is his little, forgotten acts of kindness and love. The strength of a relationship is built on the innumerable acts of kindness we perform each day. A thank-you note, a card on an old friend's birthday, an unexpected back rub—these are the actions that really communicate how we feel about another person.

• *Don't jump to conclusions.*

We often theorize on someone else's behavior and begin to treat that theory as fact. For instance, say you're supposed to meet a friend for dinner. Your friend is late showing up. You start to get angry. How inconsiderate, you think. This person obviously has no regard for your feelings. They must think very little of you if they don't care about being on time for your appointment. At last, your friend shows up, looking tired and disheveled. They had a car accident on the way to the restaurant. Now that you know the facts, how do you feel?

When you begin to act on your assumptions, you run the risk of closing your mind to facts, offending the other person, and making grave mistakes. If you have ever done any coaching, you know when a player is not performing to his or her usual level, your first tendency is to come up with a reason, or hypothesis, to explain the problem. The explanation could be something as simple as an undetected injury or as complicated as a family or personal problem. Still, as a coach, you need to be careful that you don't jump to the wrong conclusion and, thus, delay solving the problem.

- *The noes make the yeses count.*

Athletes, with all their successes, have great difficulty with being told no. It seems like losing. It is part of competition to neither give up nor never give in—in other words, to never take no for an answer. If, however, a person in a relationship with you can't say no to you, then their yeses don't count for much because they are not freely given. In a good relationship, both partners must feel comfortable enough to give and accept the word no. In that difficult period when I was getting reacquainted with my wife, I heard a lot of noes. In the long run, though, the yeses began to count.

- *Make the relationship your top priority.*

Any time your relationship isn't moving forward, it's moving backward. It's like muscle tone—use it or lose it! Many of us begin to take our relationships for granted. We'll spend hours a week maintaining our economic fitness, but our personal relationships get whatever time is left over (which usually isn't much).

- *Continue the courtship.*

More marriages die at the altar than anywhere else. Why? Because once couples say "I do," they *don't*! Don't court, that is. With every couple I've worked with in my years of marriage counseling, I've sought to reintroduce the concept of courtship. I've urged them to start dating each other again. With that weekly Friday night date comes the renewed realization that they're with each other because they want to be, not because there's nothing better to do.

• *Get the big picture.*

One of the reasons John Wooden could build his UCLA basketball dynasty was because he thought conceptually, as well as operationally. That is, not only did he focus on the daily, nuts-and-bolts aspect of coaching, he could also see his team and their competition in the larger sense—as part of a league, as part of a national championship.

Seeing how daily actions affect the broader aspects of our lives is what I call getting the "big picture." Not to pick on men, but it's been my experience that men have a problem getting the big picture in their relationships. They say, "I don't understand why my wife's so mad at me. So she asked me to do something and I forgot it. It's not like I'm an ax murderer or anything!"

The point isn't that a husband forgets to pick up his wife's dress at the cleaners. Rather, if it had been his suit at the cleaners, his wife would have, likely, gone out of her way to pick it up—without having to be asked. Yet not only did hubby have to be asked, he then turned around and showed exactly how important it was to him by forgetting something *important* to his wife. Men need to be better at getting the big picture. They need to look beyond actions, to the meaning of those actions.

• *A relationship can't tolerate two crazy people at the same time.*

I refereed men's college basketball for 15 years. During that time, we referees were always concerned about the possibility of trouble breaking out on the floor. Our job was to spot potential problems and stop them before they started. If we saw an overly aggressive foul committed, we jumped in and called the foul to reassure everyone that the situation was under control. This was supposed to reduce the likelihood of any player taking matters into his own hands and retaliating. A couple of times, though, we weren't fast enough and both teams rushed out on the floor, pushing and even slugging each other.

The same thing (usually minus the pushing and slugging) happens all the time in relationships. One person's irrationality or unreasonableness triggers the other person's irrationality, and then you have trouble. That's why, if the other person "goes crazy," you have to take responsibility for keeping yourself under control. Two crazy people at the same time is what causes serious harm to a relationship.

• *Being right isn't as important as you think it is.*

I've spent thousands of hours trying to help people resolve interpersonal conflicts. Most of the time, conflict is over who is right and who is wrong—not on how the situation can be resolved. Sometimes you need to ask yourself if being right is important enough to create distance between you and the other person. Sometimes it is. Most of the time it isn't.

• *Sharing your thoughts is always important.*

In his book, *After the Honeymoon*, Dr. Daniel B. Wile says that the key ingredient in a strong and happy marriage is the ability of both partners to say what they need to say in a way that the other will understand. There's an old saying, "Trouble shared is trouble halved." That's certainly true in a marriage. Problems that are discussed openly usually become more manageable. As Wile says, "All couples need to have [these] discussions—and yet few couples do. As a result, many couples feel vaguely deprived. They sense that something is lacking in their relationship, and they cast about for a particular problem—such as 'incompatibility' or 'lack of common interests'—on which to pin such feelings. These couples do not realize that it is their inability to have important, intimate conversations that is causing their marital malaise."

It can be scary to open yourself up to another human being, even if that person is someone closer to you than anyone else. It can be even scarier when the feelings you're disclosing have to do with a problem in the relationship. However, I've found the risk lies not so much in expressing negative feelings, but in burying them in the hope that things will, miraculously, get better.

The foundation of all interpersonal relationships is to understand the other person before seeking to be understood. By implementing the principles I've talked about in this chapter, you will find your understanding of others will grow, and your relationships with them will improve.

## Practice Time

### Relating - Part I

Think of a past relationship that was not successful. It may have been a romantic relationship, a friendship, a relationship with a coach or teacher, etc. Using what you've learned in this chapter, analyze the relationship. Ask yourself the following:

• Did my involvement in sports contribute to the failure of this relationship? If so, how?

• What might I have done differently to improve this relationship?

### Relating - Part II

Now think of a current relationship that you would like to improve. It could be a bad relationship that you would like to save, or a good relationship you'd like to make even better. On a piece of paper, list the principles of a successful relationship that were outlined earlier in this chapter. Under each principle, write some suggestions as to how you can implement that principle in your relationship. Example:

• Take care of your own side of the street.
   Instead of criticizing my parents all the time for how they treat me, I will start treating them with more respect and consideration.

# 29
# CALLING THE PLAYS
## How to Communicate What You Want (and Learn What Others Need)

### The Game Plan

In this chapter, I will talk about:

- why effective communication is one of the most important skills you can learn
- what sports teach you about communication
- the qualities of an effective communicator
- how to improve your communication "game"
- communication's "front line": listening, selling, and negotiating

*I see communication as a huge umbrella that covers and affects all that goes on between human beings. Once a human being has arrived on this earth, communication is the largest single factor determining what kinds of relationships he makes with others and what happens to him in the world about him. How he manages his survival, how he develops intimacy, how productive he is, how he makes sense, how he connects with his own divinity—are all largely dependent on his communication skills.*
- Virginia Satir, psychologist and author

What would happen if a football team tried to execute a play without having any idea of what play was being run? Or if two outfielders tried to catch the same ball without one of them signaling for the catch?

Good communication is vital to the success of an athletic team. Even in individual sports, communication plays an important role. Tennis players, for example, need to be able "read" their opponents. This kind of communication is non-verbal, but it's communication all the same.

Players and coaches must to be able to communicate with each other to have a successful relationship. One sportswriter attributed the firing of a prominent college basketball coach to the fact that the coach simply lost the ability to communicate with his players. The resulting frustration made everyone miserable and made the team ineffective.

In many ways, sports can help you improve your communication skills, which has lifelong benefits. Being part of a team, for example, gives you the opportunity to learn to take direction and work with your peers. These are things that require you to communicate effectively.

Of course, some people are more effective communicators than others. Athletes see the results of effective communication all the time: doubles players rush the net together and win the point; a pick-off play works and a big inning is avoided; the offensive line reads the blitz and saves the quarterback from being sacked.

Athletes also see the results of ineffective communication. I can remember one such instance of miscommunication in my own life. I was playing tennis with a friend of mine, a big, powerful fellow who usually has no trouble in handling me on the court. On this particular day, however, I was leading six games to five. We were in the middle of a long rally when my friend mishit a shallow cross-court shot that, luckily for him, fell in-bound by about 10 inches. As I walked back to the end line to pick up the ball, I made a comment about the hit. Imagine my surprise when I turned around to serve, only to find my friend towering above me, obviously angry.

"What are you doing here?" I asked.

"You said I missed it," he glowered.

"Oh, no," I quickly replied. "I said you mishit. The ball was still good." With disaster averted, we returned to our game. This incident impressed upon me how easy (and how dangerous) it is to miscommunicate.

## Keys to Effective Communication

*Seek first to understand, then to be understood.*
- Stephen R. Covey

What does it take to be an effective communicator? Self-esteem tops the list. When you have positive self-esteem, you feel confident presenting your ideas or feelings to others. When you have poor self-esteem, you're less likely to open up to others and to be open to constructive criticism. People with low self-esteem often over compensate, coming across as egotistical and defensive—neither of which are conducive to effective communication.

Effective communicators know how to express themselves clearly. How many times are relationships damaged because people are unable to say what they mean in a way others understand? For example, a supervisor may tell you they want a project done as soon as possible. To you, "as soon as possible" may mean after you have finished whatever you're working on at the moment. To your supervisor, however, "as soon as possible" may mean immediately. In this situation, your supervisor's inability to clearly express when he or she wants the project done will probably cause some problems.

Effective communicators keep a cool head. Sometimes athletes (male, especially) have a problem doing this. The aggressive, egocentric, competitive nature of sports does not lend itself to conversation in the face of strong emotions. Can you imagine a batter and a pitcher having the following conversation:

| | |
|---|---|
| Batter: | Look, you almost hit me with that last ball of yours and I feel very angry about it. |
| Pitcher: | You're right. I'll try to be more careful next time. |

Not likely! Instead, the offended batter runs out to the mound, slugs the pitcher, and then both dugouts empty onto the field for a free-for-all. When this sort of behavior occurs in real life, it can be very damaging. That's why it is important for athletes to learn how to express their emotions, constructively, rather than destructively.

Effective communicators aren't afraid to share their feelings. The willingness to trust others with your feelings is part of a healthy personality, and the ability to talk truthfully and fully about yourself is an essential part of effective communication.

Effective communicators make it easy for others to communicate. Earl Nightingale, one of the country's most inspirational writers and speakers, has said that effective communication is a two-way street. Anyone can talk about themselves. The truly effective communicator talks about things in such a way that the others not only understand, but respond. Nightingale uses a tennis game to illustrate his point. An effective communicator hits the ball (the conversation topic) over the net and then waits for its return. He or she does not, however, run and jump over the net. That would certainly put an abrupt end to the game.

Effective communicators know how to make a good first impression. These impressions are very important. As Milo O. Frank says in his book, *How to Get Your Point Across in 30 Seconds or Less*:

> Do you ever think about how people judge you and about how you judge others? Your deals, jobs, money and success can all hang on first impressions. Isn't it true that with just a few words, an image is formed in your mind and in theirs, and you and they act accordingly? Often there's only time for a few words, so they had better be the right ones.

There's an old saying that you never get a second chance to make a good first impression. I once read that 80 percent of all jurors never alter their first impression of the defendant. It's scary to think that life-and-death matters can hang on something as fleeting as the image you present when you first meet someone.

We used to think it took two or three minutes to complete that first impression of a person. Now we believe it takes *seven seconds or less*. Here's how the process works: The first time you meet a person, three things happen, simultaneously. One, you notice how the person looks; second, you notice how they sound; and, third, you notice what they say.

A number of years ago, researchers at Stanford University

reached a rather amazing conclusion: Seven percent of communication results from actual words being spoken; 93 percent results from *how* we communicate: Voice tone, pitch, volume, body language.

As you can see, what you say has less impact on a first impression than how you say it. Countless motivational speakers have learned this. Thus, while it's important to "know your stuff," it's imperative to present that information in a way that people actually hear it. That's what mastering effective communication skills is all about.

## Improving Your Communication "Game"

You improve your communication the same way you improve your game—by breaking it down into specific areas on which to work. I remember counseling a college quarterback and his girlfriend. The girl was pregnant and neither one of them really knew what they wanted to do about it. Get married? Keep the baby? Drop out of school?

We broke it down over several sessions. First, I had them talk about what they each wanted. What were the issues/problems involved in achieving these desires? What were the steps they needed to take as individuals and as a couple to overcome these problems?

The very first step they needed to work on was communication. They had to freely share their feelings and listen—rather than react—to what the other said. Next, they had to commit to solving their problems. Finally, they needed to come up with a plan they both could support. By addressing their problems in small bites, this couple finally reached a solution that benefited both of them.

Libraries and bookstores are filled with volumes of material on effective communication. For the purposes of this book, however, I concentrate on the three basic aspects of communication I believe are most important. I call these the "front line" of your communication "team." A strong front line is the key to your success as a communicator.

## Flexing Your Ear Muscles

*I know you believe you understand what you think I said, but I am not sure you realize that what you heard is not what I meant.*
- anonymous

*It is impossible to overemphasize the immense need humans have to be really listened to, to be taken seriously, to be understood.*
- Paul Tournier, psychiatrist and author

Russell White, was a great back at Cal-Berkley despite his relatively small size (5 feet 11 inches, 216 pounds). One of his reasons? His ability to listen. As one of his coaches put it: "This is a very smart guy, a great listener, and maybe most important, he understands how to listen and correct his mistakes."

The athlete who doesn't know how to listen reduces his or her ability to improve. The same is true whether you're in the classroom, in the work place, or in a relationship.

Listening is more than just hearing sounds. Listening is a matter of hearing what is said, not what you want to hear. Effective listening involves four different actions:

1) hearing what is said
2) accurately interpreting what is said
3) evaluating what is said
4) and responding to the message

A doctor once said to me that, in his opinion, an accurate medical diagnosis could be made 80 to 90 percent of the time by good listening alone. But if listening is so important, why aren't we better at it?

A variety of things keep us from being good listeners. At times we're distracted. Sometimes we're biased against the person who is speaking. Most of the time, though, poor listening skills result from bad habits. Here are some of the more common ineffective listening habits:

• BAD HABIT: *Disinterest.*

You're not interested in the subject, so you don't listen to the speaker.

- BAD HABIT: *Put down.*
  You're too busy criticizing the speaker for his poor delivery to actually listen to what he's saying.

- BAD HABIT: *Instant judgment.*
  Instead of listening, you're evaluating. The speaker's barely gotten two sentences out of his or her mouth and you're already decided he/she's not worth listening to.

- BAD HABIT: *Hunting for facts.*
  You take Sergeant Friday's admonition, "Just the facts, ma'am," to heart. You only listen for the facts and principles in presentations, not the ideas and feelings that connect the facts and figures.

- BAD HABIT: *Tuning out.*
  You look like you're listening, but what you're really doing is planning your vacation to Maui. (Proper listening should actually produce tension, which is released when you understand the message the speaker is delivering.)

Being a good listener is hard work. The athlete who bench presses 200 pounds without breaking a sweat may be surprised to discover just how much effort is required to listen, properly. The more you listen, the more you learn. That's what listening is really all about.

I've come up with six critical skills, or techniques, to help you become a better listener. You can think of them as listening "exercises." Do them every day, and I guarantee that your ear muscles will be as toned as the rest of your body.

### Listening Exercises

1) *Pay attention.*
A father and his young son were at a football game. The boy asked if he could get a hot dog. His father, engrossed in the action on the field, said, "Be quiet. I'm watching the game." Pretty soon, the boy asked again if he could go. His dad brushed him off by saying, "Wait a minute, please." The boy waited for what

he estimated was a minute, then slipped away in the direction of the concession stand. He was halfway there before his father caught up with him. The dad was angry because his son had left his seat without permission. The son was upset because, in his eyes, he had done what his dad asked. He had waited "a minute" before leaving.

There are two major listening problems in this case:

(1) The father wasn't paying attention.

(2) The father was teaching his child it's okay to be indifferent to someone who's speaking to you.

Before you can really listen to someone, you've got to be paying attention. Make the conscious decision that you will listen to a speaker. Clear your mind of whatever might distract you from receiving the person's message. It won't be easy. People think four to seven times faster than they talk, which is why we end up tripping over our tongues sometimes, and why our minds get bored waiting for someone else to finish his or her sentence or thought.

*2) Be supportive.*

Being a good listener means showing the speaker that you are listening. How do you do that? With supportive gestures, such as nodding your head, smiling or frowning, leaning forward, making eye contact, and so on. As a companion to support gestures, we also have support noises, which are all those encouraging little "uh huh's," "mmm's," and "I see's," that act as nudges to keep people talking.

*3) Learn to paraphrase.*

Paraphrasing means repeating what was just said, only in a different way, to insure that you have really understood what the person meant. When you state in your own words what a remark means to you, the other person can determine whether he or she is getting his or her message across. Here's an example:

He (concerned):     I think we should see other people.
She (alarmed):      You mean you want to break up?
He (worried):       No, that's not what I meant!

| She (relieved): | Oh, you think we're getting too serious too fast, and you want to slow down a little? |
|---|---|
| He (more relieved): | Yes, that's it exactly. |

4) *Ask questions.*

When you really listen to a person, you want to learn as much from them as possible. That might mean assisting the speaker by asking questions that will help you better understand them. These kind of questions are called "open" questions. An open question requires more than a simple "yes" or "no" for an answer. The best kind of open questions are those that make a person think. For example:

What do you think about this?

What do you have in mind?

What do you mean by such and such?

5) *Be quiet.*

Silence—simply waiting and saying nothing—may be the single most useful tool in coaching, counseling, and relationships of any kind. Silence gives the speaker time to think things through. Some people don't think of silence as a tool because they want to impress others with their knowledge or advice. They talk over any reflection that may be going on, thus, implying that their thoughts are more important than the speaker's.

6) *Call time-out.*

Sometimes, in order to effectively listen to another person, you need to stop listening for a while. This is usually the case when you're hearing something you really don't want to hear, such as that time-honored statement: "You're a nice person, but I just want to be friends." Before you know it, your emotions prevent you from truly hearing what the speaker says, and you're unable to formulate a rational response. This is when you need to call "time- out," to take a walk and cool off before you start communicating again.

The thing to remember about listening is not to take it for granted. You can never be "good enough" as a listener. It's like playing golf—you'll never get a perfect score, but you can improve steadily.

## Everyone Sells

*The man remembered thinking when he was in college, "Perhaps if I can learn to sell well, then I will do well in whatever I undertake."*
- from *The One-Minute Sales Person*, by Spencer Johnson, M.D., and Larry Wilson

Where would Chris Evert have been without her famous two-handed grip? What would Nolan Ryan have been without his fastball? Each of these individuals developed a special tool, or skill, that took them to the top of their respective sport. Without that skill, they'd probably have been good players, but not great players.

In the real world, the skill of selling can make the difference between the "good" and the "great." In every aspect of your life, you need to sell your point of view, your attitudes, your product or services. Selling is part of how we relate to other people.

Some of the qualities that can help you become a successful athlete can also help you be a successful salesperson.

Passion is one such quality. When you're passionate about what you're selling, whether it's your views on a piece of legislation or the newest product made by your company, that passion gets you noticed.

Desire is another. George Caras, an ex-athlete who became a highly successful sales representative for IBM as well as founder of his own sales training company, once told me that he got his desire to win from sports. He said he looked for the same desire, along with the ability to react well under pressure, in his sales people.

Many people don't like thinking of themselves as a salesperson. They equate selling with pushy, obnoxious, and even unethical behavior. What selling really involves, however, is problem-solving. That's why it's important to develop your selling skills. It enables you to position yourself as a solver of problems. Everyone appreciates the person who can solve problems for them.

The key to successful selling is an attitude of service. I've observed a lot of coaches whose attitude is, "If you want to play for me, you do it my way or not at all." On the other hand, I've seen coaches who, instead of dictating to athletes, work to sell the athletes on the benefits of their approach to the game and the training required to be successful. Today's business leaders know the value of selling employees on ideas, rather than dictating to them. Successful selling is essential to creating a loyal, dedicated, and winning team.

To be an effective salesperson, you need to:

1) *Establish rapport.*

Children are instinctively good at this. They know that it's a lot easier to get something out of Mom or Dad if that parent is in a good mood. People want to feel like they're more than just the means to an end. They want to believe that you like them and have their best interests at heart.

2) *Identify the needs of the person you are trying to influence.*

Use the listening skills you learned earlier to actively listen to the meaning and feelings behind the words being said. The more actively you listen, the better chance you have of correctly identifying what the person wants.

3) *Determine the decision-making criteria.*

Say you're being recruited by a college coach. Your decision criteria may include:

• the desire to play early in your college career
• the location of the school
• the academic programs offered
• your financial needs

If the coach doesn't really talk about any of the things on your list, you probably won't attend that school. The coach has failed in his or her recruiting effort because he or she didn't bother to find out what is really important to you.

4) *Identify the outside influences.*

Usually there are other people involved who influence the person to whom you are trying to sell. You need to know who those other people are and what their position is. For example, if you're trying to talk a friend into sharing an off-campus apartment with you, your friend's parents may have a big influence on that decision. If they're concerned about such things as cost, safety, and whether you will get any studying done, then you need to address those issues—*not* that the apartment complex has a weight room, jacuzzi, and two tennis courts.

5) *Know who the decision-maker is.*

Is the person you're dealing with the one who has the power to okay the deal? In the previous example, it won't do much good to get your friend to agree if it's the parents who have the final word.

6) *Recognize resistance.*

Whenever you try to sell something, you will almost always meet with resistance. When the other person raises objections, you must strive to understand why. Maybe they need additional information, or perhaps you left some questions unanswered.

7) *Ask for what you want.*

Summon the courage to ask for what you want, whether it be love, respect, a job, or a sales order. Certainly, there is a chance you may be rejected or hurt. On the other hand, you may get what you ask for. If you have been sensitive, thoughtful, and hard-working—if you have learned what the other person's needs are and matched those needs with a solution—then you deserve a commitment. Don't be shy about asking for it!

The point to remember about selling is you can have more fun and success when you stop trying to get what you want and begin helping others get what they want. This isn't just a platitude; it's the way things really work.

## Negotiating: Going for the Win-Win

*It's said that when Moses came down from the mountain after getting the Ten Commandments, he said, "Well, we reasoned together. I got Him down to ten, but adultery's still in."*

- Harvey Mackay, *Swim with the Sharks*

Selling and negotiating go together like a ball and bat: You can have one without the other, but it's harder to play the game.

Negotiating is a skill that will help you succeed in all aspects of life. In athletic competition, there can only be one winner. In successful business and personal relationships, however, there must always be two winners: You and the other person. Making sure that both parties end up satisfied is part of the fine art of negotiation.

Negotiation is used to resolve disputes, divide resources, or settle differences between parties. According to the late Bob Woolf, an attorney who negotiated more than 2,000 contracts for professional athletes, negotiating is "about persuading someone to your point of view." Negotiating also can get you what you want when you don't think someone's going to just come out and give it to you. You conduct countless negotiations every day, in every relationship you have. When a kid promises his mom he'll take violin lessons if she lets him go out for the football team, that's negotiating. When an athlete refuses to join the team unless his salary is increased, that's negotiating.

The problem many people have with negotiating is that too many times the result of a negotiation leaves them with a bad feeling. They feel like they've given away or lost too much. That doesn't have to happen, however. Everyone can learn to be a more successful negotiator.

## Strategies for Successful Negotiating

1) *Do your homework.*

Know what your position is, what the other person's position is, what concessions you're willing to make, and what things you won't negotiate. Probably the most common mistake people make when it comes to negotiating is not doing their homework. They concentrate more on the actual meeting ("What should I wear?" "What should I say?") than on gathering facts and generating options.

2) *Understand the other side.*

People do what they do for (what seems to them) good reasons. Whether you agree with the other person or not, you need to accept his or her concern as valid. The success of any agreement is dependent on the quality of the people negotiating it. Always be sensitive, never gloat, and don't waste time trying to assess blame.

3) *Don't negotiate against yourself.*

Sometimes we're so eager to close the deal, we offer the other person more than they would have asked for. Then we end up feeling like we've lost.

4) *Practice the art of "quid pro quo."*

*"Quid pro quo"* is a Latin expression meaning "this for that." It means getting something for what we give away. People in the public eye do this all the time. They do a benefit or appear on a talk show in return for free publicity. Former athletes, like myself, practice *quid pro quo* when we volunteer to coach the local Little League or YMCA team. It lets us give something to the community, while maintaining contact with our sport.

5) *Know when to keep your mouth shut.*

Silence can be a formidable negotiating weapon. Not only does a long, silent spell during a negotiation make other people nervous, it encourages them to offer you more. It also keeps you from negotiating against yourself.

6) *Emphasize points of agreement.*

Which of these statements would you be more responsive to:

> "There's no way we can give you a 20 percent
> raise; you'll have to settle for five percent."

> - or -

> "Your performance has been excellent. You're
> one of our best team players and we'd hate to
> lose you. You certainly deserve a raise, but we
> can't afford to give you a 20 percent increase at
> this time. Could you accept five percent?"

When you emphasize the things you agree on, it makes it easier to negotiate the things you don't agree on.

7) *Avoid ultimatums.*

You should always ask for what you want, but never demand it "or else." Nobody likes to be threatened.

8) *Never give up.*

If it seems like things are stymied, try the "if-then" approach. For example, say: "If I can improve my running time by five-tenths of a second, then will you let me be a starter?" Above all, remember the lesson to be learned from the Yogi Berra School of Negotiating: It ain't over till it's over.

When negotiations fail, it's often because people have a win-lose attitude. They view negotiating more like an athletic contest. They plot strategies, figure out how to score points, hold their ground, meet to "butt heads," and hope to walk away from the negotiations victorious. They feel that once the score is settled and the results are in, the game is over.

The goals and outcomes of real-life negotiations, however, are usually far more complex. In real life, the conclusion of a negotiation is usually just the beginning. The relationship still continues.

A successful negotiator makes people feel like they're being rewarded for their cooperation. People who negotiate for the win-win realize a good decision or agreement will make both parties stronger. They know that applying this principle not only helps them achieve success in life, but also strengthens the relationship that will make that success sweeter.

## Practice Time

### Reading the Signals - Part I

To get a better idea of your communication competence, respond to the statements below with "true" or "false."

1. I use appropriate eye contact when talking.

2. I nod my head at appropriate times while the other person is talking.

3. I speak at a relaxed, controlled pace.

4. I smile appropriately when I'm talking.

5. I remain comfortably close to the person with whom I am talking.

6. I am relaxed and have comfortable posture.

7. I don't hesitate or use many vocal pauses (uh, you know, etc.) when I talk.

8. I avoid playing with objects such as a pen, paper, or silverware.

9. When the other person smiles at me, I return the smile.

10. I indicate that I understand what the other person is saying and feeling.

11. I show that I am listening by using verbal reinforcers (I see, Go on, Uh huh, Right).

12. I avoid unnecessarily interrupting the other person.

13. I make sure that we both have an opportunity to talk.

14. I don't play with my hair or clothing during conversations.

15. I listen intently, giving my undivided attention.

Review your answers. The statements that received "false" responses are areas that you need to work to improve.

## Reading the Signals - Part II

Are you a good listener? Take the following quiz to find out.

### Are You a Good Listener?

*Circle the number that best applies.*
**(5) Almost Always    (4) Usually       (3) Sometimes**
**(2) Seldom          (1) Almost Never**

1. Do you like to listen to other people talk?        5 4 3 2 1

2. Do you listen regardless of a speaker's manner
   of speech and choice of words?                      5 4 3 2 1

3. Do you listen even if you don't like who's
   talking?                                            5 4 3 2 1

4. Do you listen equally well to friend,
   acquaintance, stranger?                             5 4 3 2 1

5. Do you put what you have been doing out of
   sight and out of mind?                              5 4 3 2 1

6. Do you look at the speaker?                         5 4 3 2 1

7. Are you able to ignore distractions?                5 4 3 2 1

8. Do you smile, nod your head, and otherwise
   encourage the speaker?                              5 4 3 2 1

9. Do you think about what the speaker is saying?  5 4 3 2 1

10. Do you try to figure out why the person is
    saying it?                                         5 4 3 2 1

11. Do you let the person finish what he/she is
    trying to say?                                     5 4 3 2 1

12. If the person hesitates, do you encourage
    him/her to go on?                          5 4 3 2 1

13. Do you restate what the person says and ask
    him/her if you have the meaning right?      5 4 3 2 1

14. Do you withhold judgment about a speaker's
    idea until he/she has finished?            5 4 3 2 1

15. Do you listen even though you anticipate what
    the speaker is going to say?               5 4 3 2 1

16. Do you question the speaker in order to get
    them to explain the idea better?            5 4 3 2 1

17. Do you ask a speaker what the words mean as
    he/she uses them?                          5 4 3 2 1

Now, add up your total points and enter the figure here: _____

If you rated yourself with a score of less than 70, you need to make a serious effort to improve your listening skills.

# 30
# THE FINAL SCORE
## A Message to Parents, Coaches, and Others

### The Game Plan

In this chapter, I will talk about:

* ultimate sports experiences—what they are and how to achieve them
* the roles that parents and coaches should play in the development of an athlete
* some parting thoughts

*Ultimate sports experiences uplift the spirits of all participants; athletes, coaches, officials, and spectators, hereby performing renewal functions, not only for individuals, but for families, communities, and the larger society.*
                    - Dave Epperson, Ph.D.

Last year my good friend, Dave Epperson, and I were working on plans for the 1994 Volleyball Festival (the third largest sporting event in the world). We spent time developing our vision of what ultimate sports experiences should be. We concluded that sports at its best had little to do with who scored the most points, or had the best coaching record, or was in the stands when a record was broken. Instead, our discussion led us to the conclusion that sports fulfill their promise when they renew and uplift *all* its participants.

### Ultimate Sports Experiences

*Fun should be the ultimate goal of sports for kids; not greatness. For every kid who was driven to early success there are a thousand who grew frustrated with sports because they could not meet expectations.*
                    - David Wohl

*Perhaps the most enlightening aspect of the tournament was the upbeat nature of the players. The average weekend golfer grouses about his life, bad luck or throws clubs when a shot goes astray. The amputees take their golf seriously, but good-naturedly. They are happy merely to be playing.*

- "Game is Serious, the Real Joy is in the Playing," Mel Florence,
*Los Angeles Times*, July 1, 1991

Whether you're competing, coaching, or cheering, you should be enjoying yourself. Otherwise, why bother?

John Elway, quarterback for the Denver Broncos, said prior to the 1993-94 season he seriously considered quitting football. Conflicts with the Broncos' former head coach had taken the fun out of football. Sure, there was that $4.6 million a year salary, but that wasn't the point.

"I was making a lot of money," Elway said, "but I don't know that any amount of money is worth your personal sanity."

We live in an era when more kids sign up for organized sports than in any previous generation. Unfortunately, they also drop out of these programs in record numbers. The primary reason kids give for quitting sports is that playing simply isn't fun anymore.

Children play sports to have fun. Interest in learning and improving skills, making friends, winning, and becoming physically fit come after enjoyment.

I fear that a large number of junior high and high school athletes—boys and girls—play for scholarships and not out of love for the game. In this, they are likely fueled by their parents and coaches.

What can parents do to ensure their child's initiation into sports will spark a lifelong enjoyment of athletics? Here are some tips:

• Don't sign your child up for a sports program without first investigating the philosophy of the league or organization. (This goes for adults, too. I know of one church group that sponsors two volleyball teams—one team for down-and-dirty competitors, and one for those players who just want to have fun.)

• Don't get your child in over his head. Just because Junior falls into a certain age group, doesn't mean his developmental skills are ready for that group.

• Ask about the length of the sports season or lesson. Unless your child is aiming for the Olympics, she shouldn't be devoting the majority of her time to sports.

• Check out the reputation of the coach. Is the coach fair? Do all the players get to compete? Do the kids enjoy playing for the coach?

• Don't focus on how many competitions the child wins; focus on how much progress they make. Be sure to point this out to your child.

You can always tell which athletes are having fun. They are a joy to watch. One of the reasons fans enjoyed Magic Johnson so much was that he enjoyed basketball so much. Those who followed Magic's career from the beginning will never forget his first game with the Lakers, when he leaped into Kareem's arms after the Lakers won in the closing seconds. As the years passed and Magic matured into one of basketball's great players, he never lost that childlike joy of the game.

Win or lose, ultimate sports experiences are those that uplift the human spirit of everyone. Sports uplifts and renews when it:

1) *Provides an opportunity to test yourself...win or lose, to be the best you can be.*

**He [Coach Wooden] had faith in us as players and as people. He was about winning basketball, and winning as human beings. The consummate teacher, he taught us that doing the best you are capable of is victory enough.**

**- *Kareem*, by Kareem Abdul-Jabbar with Mignon McCarthy**

One of the things that makes the Special Olympics such a unique event is its emphasis on the achievement of each athlete. For these disabled individuals, simply competing is a cause for celebration.

For young athletes, I believe the focus of sports should be primarily on achievement. Yes, winning and losing are part of life's lessons and these things need to be learned, but they come soon enough.

In a booklet called *Child Centered Coaching*, Dr. Stephen J. Bavolek emphasizes: "Athletic contests, games and sporting events are utilized at their best when children learn the importance of teamwork, effort, and friendly spirited play. They are utilized at their worst when children feel defeated as people, quit trying to improve, and think of themselves as losers. When that happens we all lose."

It is critical that the adults involved with sports—parents, coaches, and others—show athletes (especially young ones) that what matters most is how you play the game. In an essay on competition, Mariah Burton Nelson, wrote: "It's important that we not just parrot that cliché, but demonstrate our commitment to fair, participatory competition by paying equal attention to skilled and unskilled children; by allowing all children to participate fully in games, regardless of the score; and by caring more about process than results."

Ultimate sports experiences result in participants feeling good about what they've accomplished.

## 2) *Provides opportunities to grow.*

Ultimate sports experiences help individuals grow and develop by giving them opportunities to become good at something. Some athletes become good at the actual techniques of the sport—running, jumping, kicking, or whatever. Others, at less obvious things, such as inspiring others, getting people to work together, or trying hard despite a lack of skills.

Part of a coach's job is telling athletes what to do. But it is also part of a coach's job to help athletes learn how to do things on their own. That's how people grow into competent and, thus, confident human beings.

Developing competencies is a main ingredient of Philadelphia 76ers coach John Lucas successful coaching style. Lucas puts players in charge of time-outs, has them run portions of some practices, and even lets them occasionally give the post-game talks and assess fines.

While coaching the San Antonio Spurs a few years ago, Lucas explains his strategy this way:

> They do some things they probably never thought they would do as a player. With this team, I have such smart players. I've got to keep challenging them. I don't coach this team. I manage them. I have loose reins on them until it is time to have a different plan. And the better they get, the more I let them go.
>
> ...I'm not interested in winning games. We need to build some character here, we need to build some confidence in one another and we need some trust. All the intangible things that don't go along with X's and O's.

Sports, at their best, allow athletes to develop because the competencies developed on the playing field create confidence for the bigger game of life.

People often have the mistaken notion that sports build confidence because they give athletes the opportunity to win. Sometimes parents worry that if their children don't win at sports, it will be bad for the child's self-esteem. In effect, this gives the athlete the message that you must win to feel good about yourself. But it's not winning, or being successful, that builds self-esteem. Many very successful people have had very poor self-esteem.

What builds self-esteem is the *process* of working toward a goal—the process of coping with setbacks, of struggling on when we may not feel like it, of improving when we never thought we could. When Arthur Ashe was in the final stage of his fight against AIDS, he knew that he probably wasn't going to win the battle. But he didn't let that stop him from trying, and from enjoying the fight. In his memoir he writes:

> Yes, I felt pain, physical and psychological; but I also felt something like pleasure in responding purposefully, vigorously, to my illness. I had lost many matches on the tennis court, but I had seldom quit. I was losing, but playing well now; my

head was down, eyes riveted on the ball as I
stroked it; I had to be careful but I could not be
tentative; my follow-through must flow from the
shot, fluid and smooth. Experience as an athlete
had taught me that in times of danger I had to respond with confidence, authority and calm.

One sportswriter said, "Wouldn't it be great if we could use
sport for what it is intended—to be able to grow and develop,
learn optimism and hope, fun and enjoyment? And wouldn't it
be wonderful if we had adults who are mature, sensitive and truly concerned for children directing these programs?"

When Tim Flannery's playing days with the San Diego Padres ended, he went on to take a job with the Padres as a roving
instructor and Class A manager. Flannery noted, "There are
things I want to teach the kids, other than the game of baseball."

Ultimate sports experiences provide more than just the opportunity to learn the skills of the sport. It provides an environment for growth—time to learn about leadership, tolerance, pa-
tience, and forgiveness—and it provides these opportunities to
everyone involved.

In the late 1960s and early 1970s, Jim Ryun was the world's
greatest runner. He was the first prep runner to run the mile in
under four minutes; he set world records in the mile, 880 yards,
and the 1,500 meters. Yet, three times he failed to take a gold
medal in the Olympics.

In his first Olympic, still in high school, he was too young
and inexperienced to capture a medal. In Mexico City in 1968,
Ryun came home with a silver medal after (as was discovered in
1989) the race was fixed against him. Finally, during a prelimi-
nary heat at the 1972 Olympics in Munich, Ryun was elbowed
by a competitor and fell, hitting his head against a metal guard
rail. He finished the race, but the time lost by his fall kept him
from making the finals. Another person may have been bitter,
but Jim Ryun decided to put his negative experience to positive
use. "It [the fall] became a real asset in my life," Ryun said.
"Athletes are often removed, put on a pedestal, but I was
brought back to reality."

Jim Ryun never won the gold medal that he sought. He did,

however, develop the strength of character that helped him look beyond the loss to other things that were important in his life. His athletic experience was instrumental in gaining that strength.

Ultimate sports experiences help athletes build skills and character traits that prove beneficial off the field as well as on.

Sports also let participants learn how to handle their feelings in creative and constructive ways. For example, when a team loses a hard-fought contest and manages to sincerely congratulate the winners, team members learn to handle disappointment and frustration.

Sports can help us deal with emotions caused by outside events, as well. Physical exercise, for instance, releases chemicals in the body that make a person feel good. Exercise, thus, has long been used as a prescription for people who suffer from forms of depression. Sports participation, then, is a good way to let off steam, to energize ourselves when we don't feel particularly energetic, and to simply celebrate the joy of having a body that can do so many wonderful things.

Unfortunately, athletic events are sometimes marred by people who use sports as an excuse to express feelings in a negative way. Athletes get upset and turn the field into a slugfest. Coaches scream and rant. Unruly fans pelt contestants or officials with snowballs and other debris. But perhaps worst of all is the parent whose emotions get out of control. In his memoirs, Arthur Ashe related the story of one such parent:

> We had organized an informal tennis tournament for kids staying at the resort. One boy, about eleven years old, fought hard but lost his match. He walked off the court disconsolately. I watched him go up to his father, who promptly punched him in the head. I was stunned…People like that sometimes destroy the joy of sport and the joy in the lives of young people.

More recently, one young tennis star on the women's circuit had to have a restraining order issued against her father, who was notorious for his abusive behavior toward his daughter, tennis officials, and even other fans.

Because sports are filled with drama, tension, and excitement, it is easy to get carried away. However, the ultimate sports experience will always be one that helps participants express their feelings in a positive and beneficial way.

Athletes know you can't make every shot. If you want to win, though, you have to make the shots that count. That's the way it is in the real world, too. If you can't be a success at everything (and who can?), then be a success at the things that are important.

Sadly, some of us don't realize what's important until it's too late. In 1985, Pete Rose managed to break Ty Cobb's all-time record of 4,191 hits. It took him 22 years to do it and was one of the top sports stories of the decades. It wasn't *the* top story, however. When sportswriters and broadcasters voted for the top sports story of the 1980s, Pete Rose's record-breaking accomplishment came in second. His suspension from baseball on gambling charges was first.

As I stated earlier, the ultimate sports experience is one that helps us grow and develop. It is through that growth that we come to a better understanding of ourselves. I think of one of my friends who went through grade school, junior high, and high school as an athletic dropout.

She was a straight-A student whose PE class was the bane of her existence, since she could never pull higher than a "C" in it. Then, while in college, she got interested in running. She started with one lap around the track—barely. To this day, she's not sure why she kept at it, but she did. Running became part of her daily life. Weightlifting was next. It became a new challenge, to see if the same arms that couldn't throw a baseball more than 10 yards could lift a 50-pound barbell over her head. After that came aerobics. By the time she graduated to teaching her own aerobics class, my friend knew that sports had done more than just instill in her a new sense of confidence. It was sports, more than anything else, that helped her discover her abilities for self-discipline, goal-setting, and determination. Her sports experience brought her to a better understanding of herself, and that understanding furthered her development in other areas of her life.

3) *Strengthen personal ties.*

*...I learned a long time ago what money can and cannot do for me. From what we get, we can make a living; what we give, however, makes a life.*
- Arthur Ashe, *Days of Grace*

Just when I think I can't bear to open the sports pages one more time for fear I'll read another headline about an athlete gone bad, I discover just the opposite. I read a story about a young baseball player from the streets of L.A. who plans to go back and talk to the kids who were left behind; who wants to tell them that their lives don't have to end in drugs or guns or an early death. I read about a college basketball player who risked his life to save a family trapped in a burning car. I read something like Arthur Ashe's moving memoir, *Days of Grace*, and realize that there are still plenty of athletes who are setting the example that reaching out to others is important. It's a way of sharing the positive contributions sports makes to your life.

Ultimate sports experiences have the ability to connect people. Just look at Texas and football, Indiana and basketball. Although the fans in these areas may get a little rabid at times, sports can connect them in a positive way—the way people usually only connect in times of catastrophe.

When Dan Jansen at long last speed-skated his way to Olympic gold in 1994, millions of people knew his story and cheered him on. When he won, we all felt like winners.

Sports give athletes the chance to establish satisfying relationships with a variety of individuals and groups—teammates, competitors, coaches, and supporters. What athletes gain from these relationships should inspire them to want to give something back.

This connecting with others is characterized by respect. You often hear athletes talking about respecting their opponents. In this world, you'll come in contact with many different people. You probably won't love all of them; you may not even like all of them. But an individual of character will strive to at least accord other human beings the dignity of being respected.

We learn the principle of respect through example. That

example should begin at home. Nothing shapes the future of a young athlete growing up more than the values that are learned and goals that are established through the inspiration and encouragement provided by the moms and dads of the community.

Parents teach their children respect when they:

- Let the child play whatever sport he/she chooses
- Teach the child to respect the coach
- Are willing to let the child make mistakes and learn from them
- Are interested/supportive/understanding/accepting/tolerant of the child
- Are willing to be flexible with their own opinions

Parents show their children that respect *isn't* important when they:

- Cheat
- Ignore the rules
- Are too forceful ("making" them do this or that)

The way parents behave at their children's athletic events goes a long way toward teaching their children how to behave respectfully on and off the field.

Coaches, too, are instrumental in teaching athletes the principle of respect. Sometimes they do this by reverse example. Lou Campanelli, the basketball coach at Cal Berkeley, was fired largely because of an abrasive and combative style in dealing with his players. The firing caused a major flap. Many coaches thought it was a sign that the players were running the team. I believe, though, the issue was one of respect. The administrator who fired Campanelli explained:

> ...The words that were used were "losers," "cowards," "no guts." So many four-letter words you couldn't believe it. Now I know that is somewhat standard fare in sports today, but it's one thing to say "WE didn't play well"...or "WE played like a bunch of bleepin' losers." But when it becomes "YOU are a bunch of 'bleepin

losers." "JOHN SMITH is a bleepin' worthless coward,"...a line has been crossed and it can't be tolerated.

When coaches scream at a player for making a mistake (or hit a player, as some do), they are often considered to be great competitors. People excuse their behavior by saying it's their competitive fire expressing itself. However, I believe that a true competitor is someone who tries their best, while acting their best. This is the kind of behavior coaches should strive for in themselves and in their players. This is part of ultimate sports experiences.

## A Final Message to Parents and Coaches

In discussing this book project with legendary basketball coach John Wooden, I asked if he thought sports build character. He replied, "It can ... or it can tear it down. It all depends on leadership."

The story is told of Mel Blount, who went from being a poor, barefoot farm boy to a star defensive player for the Pittsburgh Steelers. Near the end of his career, Blount found himself pondering a question that Steeler coach Chuck Noll had raised in a locker-room speech: "Football isn't everything. What will be your life's work?"

For Blount, the answer to that question came from talking to some of his young fans—youth who grew up without the values and stability he received from his own family. Blount decided that helping these boys would be his "life's work." He went on to establish a licensed youth home—a farm similar to the one he had grown up on—where neglected and abused kids could learn the values of hard work, pride, and responsibility.

It is essential for an athlete to find purpose and meaning off the field as well as on, and sometimes it requires the guidance of a parent or coach to help the athlete find that purpose. Too often, however, that guidance is lacking.

Is it too much to expect a coach or parent to take five minutes after an athletic event and say, "OK, what did you learn?

How can you apply this to everyday life?" True, ultimately, the responsibility of looking for and implementing the positive lessons of sports lies with the athlete. Still, other people *are* involved, most notably, parents and coaches. Because the athlete may be caught up in performance, their most important role is providing perspective—a bridge between what they are doing on the field and what is necessary in the field of their lives.

Before parents can help their children get the most out of the sports experience, they must first ask themselves what they expect their children to get from sports.

Next, parents must be clear about their own role. Parents who are secretly hoping that Junior will either (a) carry on the family jock tradition, or (b) be the jock that dear old mom or dad never was, are usually setting themselves and their child up for disappointment.

At the opposite end of the spectrum are those parents who don't involve themselves at all in their child's athletic endeavors. This can be as harmful as the parent who gets *too* involved. Not only does it show a lack of concern on the parent's part, but it also means the child might miss out on learning some of the valuable lessons of sports. It is important that parents be available to help their kids learn the lessons we discussed earlier in this book. Through such guidance, parents can better ensure that their children's sports experience is a positive and enjoyable one.

And what of the coach's role in a player's development? In the August 1988 issue of the *Journal of Physical Education, Recreation and Dance*, John Massengale, director of the School of Health, Physical Education, and Recreation at the University of Nevada-Las Vegas, and UNLV sociology professor James Frey wrote that school sports and the teaching personnel associated closely with them (primarily, coaches) educate participants in a "dysfunctional manner." In other words, the things players are taught are not what they need to learn to be healthy, contributing members of society.

With all the positive lessons sports can promote, why is it that some coaches and athletic personnel aren't teaching these things? I can think of three reasons:

1) Too often, coaches live in a world that has little relationship to the real world. A coach can easily fall into the habit of

doing and saying things that seem to please himself or herself alone without regard to the feelings or development of the athletes for whom the coach is responsible.

2) Coaching is one of the few professions (and the only profession in a university setting) where no national certification standards exist. This makes it harder for coaches to be supervised and evaluated.

3) Too many coaches are in the Dark Ages when it comes to their coaching style. The most predominant style of coaching still seems to be based on the military model of "command and control." Instead, coaching should be the process of enabling others to act. It should build on people's strengths. To coach is to facilitate, which literally means to make easy—not less demanding, exciting, or intense, but less discouraging and less controlling.

Management guru Peter Drucker said, "A leader has to be an energizer and motivator, someone who inspires and guides others, who energizes the system and generates the magic that makes everyone want to do something extra."

It's important for coaches to ask themselves why it is they want to be a coach. Do they want to teach athletes the proper attitudes about sports, competition, winning, and losing? Or do they want the sense of power and control they feel they'll gain from coaching? Do they see coaching as a way to "get back in the game?" Or is it a way to share their love of the game? Finally, coaches must ask themselves if they have "the big picture" when it comes to coaching. Do they see their job as one of developing good human beings, or merely good players?

Next to parents (and sometimes even more than parents), coaches have the ability to influence athletes for better or worse. Every coach should strive to make that influence for better. In that respect, they should follow the example of Hank Iba, the second all-time winningest coach in NCAA history.

When Iba, also known as "The Godfather of College Coaching," died, Oklahoma State basketball coach Eddie Sutton eulogized him as "...a father figure to all the players that played for him. He tried to teach us what it would take to be successful when we left school by lessons on the basketball court—loyalty, discipline, hard work, things like that."

In the final score, parents, coaches, and the people who are closely involved with athletes have a responsibility to those athletes that goes beyond teaching them the lessons of the game. They need to remember to teach them the lessons of life, the lessons of humanity; the lessons that *matter*. That's what leadership is all about.

## Parting Shots

*Among the more than 25 million Americans watching the National Collegiate Athletic Association basketball tournament on television this week will be Tom Scates, the 6 foot 10 inch former Georgetown University center. A 1979 graduate, he was once a mainstay of a winning team, and his hopes were pinned on making the pros. Today he is in uniform all right—as a doorman at a downtown Washington hotel. A gentle Goliath with a cavernous bass voice and ready smile, he wears a pith helmet and has a whistle dangling around his neck to summon cabs. "There's more to life than sports," he says. "It's a hard reality."*
    - "Foul!" *TIME*, April 3, 1989

Arthur Ashe said that when he spoke to groups of young people, he tried to speak his own experience; he tried to teach them something important about life as he had learned from it.

That is what I have hoped to do with this book. My sports experience was one of the highlights of my life. It also brought me much pain and suffering—the majority of which could have been avoided if I had only known then what I know now.

Your athletic experience, whether it be Little League or professional sports, can lay a foundation for the rest of your life—but whether that foundation is positive or negative is up to you. Life in the real world will have a lot to do with what you get out of sports. Sports have the potential to add or subtract from your fulfillment in life.

As I wrote this book, I had three main objectives in mind:

• to call attention to that which is good in sports
• to prevent dropouts from life because of sports
• to  prepare athletes for the rest of their lives by identifying and extracting from sports the lessons and skills that will enhance their efforts off the playing field, and the values that build character

Julius Erving (Dr. J) once remarked, "I don't strive for superstardom.  Ironically, I never strove for superstardom in basketball.  What I strive for is to be whole, to be complete, to fully experience life.  You want to help your children gain an understanding of life itself."

I believe sports can help us gain that understanding.  As Confucius said: "I read and I forget, I see and I remember, I *do* and I understand."  Sports is hands-on experience in a lot of ways.  That experience is what teaches us about life.

As Alex Kroll stated in *The Name of the Game is Life*, "The same sport that leaves scars on your knees, leaves patterns in your mind."

In a nationwide survey of 1,865 high school students conducted in 1990, a third to a half said playing sports had no effect on other aspects of their personal lives.  These are the athletes who are not learning the lessons sports have to offer.

Indiana University basketball coach Bobby Knight said, "It's almost like one of those gigantic puzzles that takes forever to put together, and perhaps you never do.  Basketball as a game has always fascinated me, and maybe more now than ever before."  He was talking about basketball, but isn't this really what life is—a gigantic puzzle?  Sports, when it does its job, should prepare you to be better able to put the pieces together.

I do not want to be numbered among those people who are for abolishing sports programs from the school curriculum.  I am not one of those parents who would take pride in boasting that you'd never see their son or daughter taking part in barbaric athletic rituals.  Rather, my sympathies lie with those of Arthur Ashe when he counseled his daughter Camera to learn at least two "life sports"—those she could play long after she left school:

> Sports are wonderful; they can bring you
> comfort and pleasure for the rest of your life.

Sports can teach you so much about yourself, your emotions and character, how to be resolute in moments of crisis and how to fight back from the brink of defeat. In this respect, the lessons of sports cannot be duplicated easily; you quickly discover your limits but you can also build self-confidence and a positive sense of yourself. Never think of yourself as being above sports.

(from *Days of Grace*, Alfred A. Knopf, New York, 1993)

Sports *are* wonderful. And being successful as an athlete on any level is truly remarkable, but it shouldn't be considered life's greatest achievement. All the athletic success Ty Cobb attained did not keep him from becoming an unhappy person; all the athletic success Pete Rose attained did not keep him from going to prison, and all the athletic success Hank Gathers attained did not keep him from dying.

There's more to life than sports and there's more to winning than numbers on a scoreboard. I am reminded of DeAnna Sodoma, who lost her ability to walk and went on to become a champion wheelchair racer. She said, "When you see that you've lost everything and you see that you're still surviving, you're dealing with it. Well, then you realize that if you can deal with that, you can deal with anything."

As I look back on my life as a player, coach, and parent, the victories we shared were not on the field. For the most part, who won or lost has long faded from our minds. But the little things we learned about ourselves and about life are the things this book has sought to capture. The richness, the lessons, and the value of sports are indelibly printed on this scoreboard.

When Roy Campanella died of a heart attack at age 71, after spending the last 35 years of his life in a wheelchair, one writer commented, "He had been a great ballplayer, one of the best ever at his position. But in the final analysis, he was an even better human being." Isn't that what we all should be aiming for?

# AFTERWORD

"If I had known then what I know now, how different my life would have been."

How often have we heard this tired old phrase? In darker moments, we may even have uttered it ourselves.

It is, however, a phrase that need never be repeated by young athletes who read Dr. Selleck's extraordinary book. Armed with the insights it contains, they will have the information they need *now* in order to lead happy, successful lives long after the cheering has stopped.

The theme of the book centers around a question that all athletes ultimately have to ask themselves: "What do I really want to get out of sports?"

"Easy," many youngsters may say, as numerous professional athletes have said in the past. They want to shoot for fame. Or fortune. Or the thrill of winning. Or maybe just the camaraderie of being around other teammates.

While these goals are understandable, they are traps, says Dr. Selleck. And he knows, perhaps better than almost anyone else in the world, how to avoid these traps and take full advantage of the unique and lasting benefits the sports experience has to offer.

I know that coaches talk all the time about meeting the challenge of sports, both on and off the field. And, as they know only too well, this is an increasingly difficult task in this day and age. Finding and keeping good athletes, helping them deal with the academic as well as the athletic side of sports, guiding them personally as well—it is a *monumental* task. These coaches, as well as school administrators and community leaders, will all find Dr. Selleck's book of enormous help.

It is, in fact, a book for everyone who wants to understand the place sports has in our lives, and what the entire experience means to us, our families, and our loved ones.

As a personal reference, I would like to say that I am particularly moved by Dr. Selleck's book because of my own intimate involvement with competitive sports, virtually all of my adult life. I know first-hand the challenges, the temptations, and the pitfalls that are all part of the sports experience—all of which are difficult to see sometimes when the game is in progress. Thus, I am grateful to have this book as a singular road map, for myself, and for all the many people who have chosen sports as a way of helping to shape their lives and personal identity.

To that end, I would strongly urge that you keep this book nearby all the time, for quick reference, and for inspiration as well. Dr. Selleck, who was an outstanding collegiate basketball and baseball player himself, pinpoints precisely what every athlete goes through in a life of sports. No other book has traced the cycle quite as accurately, or as memorably.

*How to Play the Game of Your Life* is, in short, vital reading. Thank you, George, for getting it all down on paper.

*Rick Wolff*
*Noted sports psychologist and author*

# MORE ABOUT
# GEORGE A. SELLECK, PH.D.

George A. Selleck, Ph.D., is a national seminar and workshop leader, and has served as a management consultant to a number of prominent CEO's. He has presented business, athletic, and personal growth seminars to hundreds of organizations including: The NBA Rookie Transition Program, the American Basketball Coaches' Association, the American Football Coaches' Association, the U.S. Tennis Association, the annual Volleyball Festival for women, and to the coaching staffs of over 60 NCAA member institutions. Corporate seminar clients have included ITT, Hewlett Packard, Dow Chemical, Control Data, Southern California Edison, and Oklahoma Gas and Electric.

Dr. Selleck has recently used his extensive background as a psychologist and educator to create *Champions for Life*, a sports and life skills program for young athletes, their parents, coaches, counselors, teachers, and school administrators.

While at Compton (CA) High School, Selleck was designated the CIF High School Basketball Player of the Year. At Stanford University, he was named to the college basketball All American Team, and later to the Stanford University Basketball Hall of Fame. A former coach at Stanford University and Brentwood High School in Los Angeles, he was twice named the *Los Angeles Times* High School Coach of the Year.

# AUTHOR'S NOTE

Like those he advises, the author aims to continue learning. If you have comments or suggestions for future editions of *How to Play the Game of Your Life*, please write:

George Selleck
1764 Pala Lake Drive
Fallbrook, CA 92028

Your input is important. Thank you.

# YOU'VE READ THE BOOK. NOW JOIN THE WORKSHOPS.

**For young athletes and anyone involved
with their development–both on and off the playing field.**

Created by Dr. George Selleck, this groundbreaking series of workshops is designed to help students, parents, coaches, educators, and community leaders work together toward a common goal: to help young athletes use the sports experience to become winners in life.

For information regarding availability of the workshops in your area, call this toll-free number:

**Call 1-800-320-1538**